W9-BNB-904

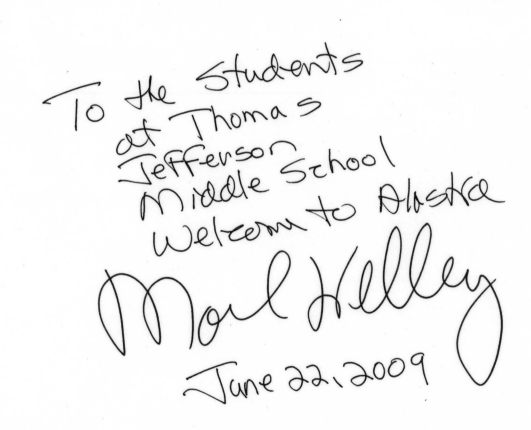

To the Students
at Thomas
Jefferson
Middle School
Welcome to Alaska

Mark Welley

June 22, 2009

ALASKA

ALASKA

A PHOTOGRAPHIC EXCURSION

Southeast Alaska · Prince William Sound · Denali National Park

Photography by MARK KELLEY

Narration by NICK JANS

Mark Kelley: photographer, publisher and project producer

Nick Jans: narrator

Laura Lucas: book and cover design

Charity Green: assistant to Mark Kelley

David Riccio, Lemon Creek Digital: scans and color management

Terra Dawn Parker: scans and color management

Paula Cadiente: proof reader

Karey Cooperrider: proof reader

Nancy Thomas: proof reader

Samhwa Printing Company, Seoul, Korea: printers

Single copies of *Alaska: A Photographic Excursion* cost $34.95 for a
hard cover edition and $24.95 for paperback plus $5.00 for shipping.
Retail discounts are available for booksellers.

BCH 8 49

Mark Kelley can be reached at PO Box 20470, Juneau, AK 99802;
by phone: toll free number (888) 933-1993 or (907) 586-1993;
by FAX: (907) 586-1201; or by email: photos@markkelley.com;
Web site: www.markkelley.com

Photographs copyright 2007 by Mark Kelley. No part of this publication
may be reproduced, stored in a retrieval system, or transmitted in any
form or by any means, electronic, mechanical, photocopying, recording
or otherwise, without the prior written permission of the publisher.

Printed in Korea
First printing December 2006
Second printing December 2007
Third printing December 2008

Hard cover edition ISBN: 978-1-57833-358-5
Paperback edition ISBN: 978-1-57833-359-2

Photos:
cover: Mt. McKinley/Denali and Wonder Lake, Denali National Park
back: Mendenhall Glacier
half-title page: Bald eagle
title page: Fairweather Range sunrise, Glacier Bay National Park
opposite page: Float plane over Juneau Ice Field
table of contents: Mt. McKinley/Denali and Nugget Pond, Denali National Park

Contents

ALASKA

A PHOTOGRAPHIC EXCURSION

Photography by MARK KELLEY   *Narration by* NICK JANS

ALASKA TRULY LIVES UP TO ITS BILLING as the Great Land, a landscape so vast and varied that it seems beyond the scale of human comprehension. Superimposed on a map of the lower 48, this largest of all states stretches from Jacksonville, Florida, to San Jose, California—mountain ranges, forests, ice fields, tundra plains, lakes and rivers rolling off to an infinite horizon. Alaska's total coastline (including its thousands of islands) is enough to circle the globe one and a quarter times. After spending a combined six decades here, Mark and I have figured one thing out: we're never going to be able to show it all.

But thanks to modern transportation and a well-placed visitor infrastructure, some of the most spectacular landscapes in Alaska are comfortably accessible. Wildlife viewing, sport fishing, and cultural opportunities abound as well. This book will take you through the Alaska the vast majority see—the coastal rain forests, fishing towns, and ice fields of Southeast Alaska; the glacier-carved landscape of Prince William Sound and Kenai Fjords;

through the major cities of Anchorage and Fairbanks; and on to the crown jewel, Denali National Park. The one truly remote area we're including is the Arctic National Wildlife Refuge. The decades-long controversy over oil development on its coastal plain has propelled this remote, pristine landscape into the national spotlight, and so it's worthy of special note.

In the process, we've left out dozens of gorgeous, worthwhile destinations across the state. In no way do we mean to slight the timeless expanse of the central and western Brooks Range; the dynamic southwestern coast, with its monster brown bears and huge salmon runs; the exotic, remote Pribilof and Aleutian Islands; the gargantuan sprawl of the Alaska Range that reaches far beyond Denali National Park—and other places, each truly deserving an entire book of its own. Our offering is a mere sampler of the state's riches, one we hope will bring you back, wanting more. All told, it's a dazzling journey.

⌐ Nick Jans

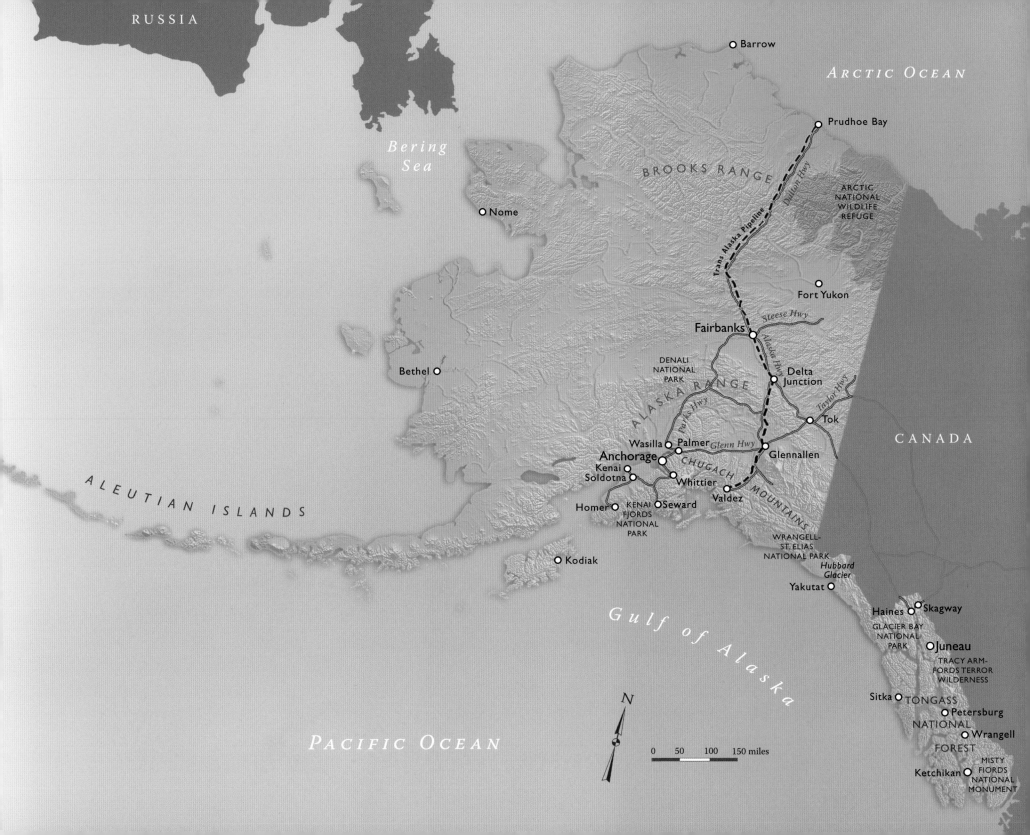

RUSSIA

*Bering
Sea*

ARCTIC OCEAN

○ Barrow

○ Prudhoe Bay

BROOKS RANGE

Dalton Hwy

Trans Alaska Pipeline

ARCTIC
NATIONAL
WILDLIFE
REFUGE

○ Nome

○ Fort Yukon

Steese Hwy

Fairbanks ○

Alaska Hwy

○ Bethel

DENALI
NATIONAL
PARK

Delta ○
Junction

Taylor Hwy

ALASKA RANGE

Parks Hwy

○ Tok

CANADA

Wasilla ○ ○ Palmer *Glenn Hwy*

Anchorage ○ ○ Glennallen

Kenai ○
Soldotna ○

CHUGACH

○ Whittier

Homer ○
KENAI
FJORDS
NATIONAL
PARK

○ Seward

Valdez ○

MOUNTAINS

WRANGELL-
ST. ELIAS
NATIONAL PARK

*Hubbard
Glacier*

A L E U T I A N   I S L A N D S

○ Kodiak

○ Yakutat

Haines ○ ○ Skagway

GLACIER BAY
NATIONAL
PARK

○ **Juneau**

TRACY ARM-
FORDS TERROR
WILDERNESS

Gulf of Alaska

Sitka ○ TONGASS

○ Petersburg

NATIONAL

○ Wrangell

FOREST

PACIFIC OCEAN

N

0   50   100   150 miles

Ketchikan ○

MISTY
FIORDS
NATIONAL
MONUMENT

Southeast Alaska

FLOAT PLANE FLIGHT OVER MISTY FIORDS

SOUTHEAST ALASKA

SOUTHEAST ALASKA IS A PARADOXICAL LAND—both harsh and benign, verdant and barren, defined equally by the life-giving power of water and the destructive force of ice. Viewed from above, it seems an impressionistic jumble—a maze of tidal waterways and literally thousands of islands hugging a mountainous coast. Dense forests of spruce, hemlock, and cedar cloak the lower slopes that rise from rocky shores; higher up, trees give way to alpine tundra, barren rock, and wild, seldom-visited ice fields where annual snowfall is measured in dozens of feet. The latter, along with the spectacular glaciers that drain them, are the remnants of a mile-thick sheath of ice that, as recently as 12,000 years ago, enveloped the region, its weight so great that the bedrock itself bowed downward. To understand the Southeast Alaska of today, you have to step back in time and envision this titanic, frozen flood, bordered by a sea 1,000 feet lower. As the ice sheets receded here and worldwide, water levels rose,

creating the network of fjords, straits, and so-called "canals" (natural rather than man-made). Most of the islands we see are merely the tops of drowned mountains, and their ancient valley floors are now the haunts of salmon, king crab, and halibut.

For travelers from the lower 48, this most southerly region of Alaska offers the advantage of proximity; it begins just 680 miles north of Seattle and stretches north another 400. This oblong chunk of real estate sprawls down the coast, forming the so-called Panhandle to the enormous "skillet" of Alaska proper. Bordered to the east by Canada's Yukon Territory and British Columbia, its eclectic mixture of place names—Baranof; San Fernando; Prince of Wales; Chilkat, and Angoon, for example—were determined by 18th century Russian, Spanish, and English explorers, and the vigorous Tlingit, Tsimshian, and Haida cultures that preceded them.

(preceding pages 10-11) Moonset over Bucareli Bay, Prince of Wales Island

A rainbow frames a salmon power troller in Cross Sound.

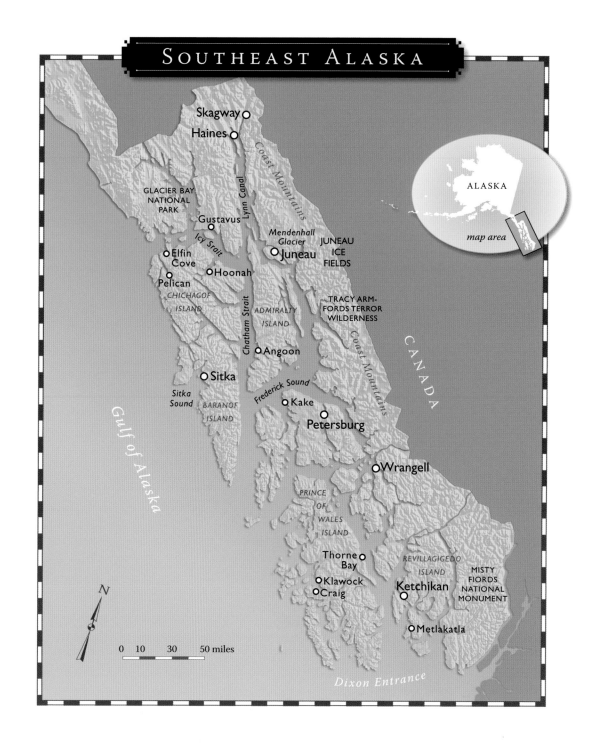

ALASKA

map area

Skagway

Haines

Coast Mountains

GLACIER BAY
NATIONAL
PARK

Lynn Canal

Gustavus

Icy Strait

*Mendenhall
Glacier*

JUNEAU
ICE
FIELDS

Elfin
Cove

Juneau

Hoonah

Pelican

*CHICHAGOF
ISLAND*

Chatham Strait

*ADMIRALTY
ISLAND*

TRACY ARM-
FORDS TERROR
WILDERNESS

Coast Mountains

CANADA

Angoon

Sitka

*Sitka
Sound*

*BARANOF
ISLAND*

Frederick Sound

Kake

Petersburg

Gulf of Alaska

Wrangell

*PRINCE
OF
WALES
ISLAND*

*REVILLAGIGEDO
ISLAND*

Thorne
Bay

MISTY
FIORDS
NATIONAL
MONUMENT

Klawock

Craig

Ketchikan

N

Metlakatla

0   10   30   50 miles

Dixon Entrance

*(left) A camper carrying a tent over his head searches for a
campsite in the West Arm of Glacier Bay National Park.*

Totem Bight State Historical Park, Ketchikan

Captain James Cook, Juan Perez, and Alexei Chirikof were among the early European visitors. All explored and mapped; but the Russians returned and stayed, building a trading empire on the pelts of sea otters and seals, and on the backs of subjugated Natives. When Alaska was sold by the czar to the U.S. in 1867 for a paltry 7.2 million dollars, the Panhandle was part of the deal. Since then, gold rushes, fishing, and timber have all played a role in the region's development; over the past decades tourism has emerged as Southeast's most important industry. The remarkable landscape as a whole, rather than any of its extractable riches, has proven to be the greatest resource of all. While the towns of Southeast are destinations in themselves, they're also jumping-off points for accessing the wild, untrammeled space that surrounds them.

Despite its rich human history, Southeast Alaska remains sparsely settled. One way of putting it: only Juneau, the state capital, can claim its human population outnumbers that of bald eagles in the region (roughly 32,000 people to 20,000 eagles). The next largest municipalities, Ketchikan and Sitka, are each around a third Juneau's size. Petersburg, Haines, and Wrangell complete the roster of towns with populations between 2-4,000; dozens of smaller communities, some bustling, some tranquil and secluded, lie scattered across the region.

High tide in Hammer Slough, Petersburg

SOUTHEAST ALASKA

As the spell of ice recedes, water has emerged as the shaping force in Southeast. The region lies at the heart of the world's largest temperate rain forest. Great waves of wet, moist air wash in from the North Pacific, rising and condensing as they break against the Coast Mountains. Local, cloud-catching topography drenches some areas in more than 200 inches a year. Half that amount is more typical, and some places receive far less. Nonetheless, a luminous, moisture-laden atmosphere defines the region—fog, clouds, drizzle, showers, and downpours alternating for days, even weeks, on end. Winters are relatively mild, with periods of snow and rain trading off; temperatures seldom fall below zero. If you hit a brilliant sunny patch (fairly common in summer, but possible anytime) consider yourself lucky. But don't shake your fist at the weather gods; instead, embrace the wet as part of the experience. What's a rain forest without rain? The restless flow of water shapes this land, raindrop to rivulet to crashing waterfall. The lush, glowing growth is fueled by it; salmon, sea lions, bears, whales, and eagles all depend on the rich flood of nutrients washing off the land, setting off huge blooms of plankton that drive the entire ecosystem. Salmon returning to their natal streams to spawn and die complete the cycle, their bodies fertilizing the waters themselves, the gargantuan Sitka spruce that line rivers and streams, the profusion of wildflowers, and the grasses on which blacktail deer feed.

A voyage through Southeast immerses the traveler in the landscape as few journeys do. The tide-swept passages between islands and mainland swirl with life, narrowing at times until the mountains lean overhead. Fishing boats surge against the current; salmon leap; a glacier looms out of the mist. Southeast's beauty and scenic riches seem infinite as they flow past.

(left) Fort William H. Seward and Chilkat Mountains, Haines

Old-growth forest, Funter Bay, Admiralty Island

Chum or dog salmon in Gold Creek, Juneau

Rare Giants

The Tongass, the largest national forest in the U.S., covers an area more than three-quarters the size of Maine. Though it's best known for stands of centuries-old Sitka spruce up to ten feet in diameter, such giants, known to forest managers as "high-volume old growth" and to loggers simply as "punkins," have never been common. Currently they make up just five percent of the Tongass.

Brown bear at forest's edge, Admiralty Island

Summertime Jewels

From the warm days of early May through late August, Southeast Alaska blazes with an ever-shifting pageant of wildflowers and berries. The yellow of skunk cabbage glows in shadowy wetlands among the last patches of snow; sun-loving lupine, irises, salmonberries, and chocolate lilies give way to Indian celery and wild geraniums as the first blueberries ripen. Meadows of fireweed count down the fading days of summer as their gaudy blossoms move ever higher up the stalk.

Columbine, Admiralty Island

(left) Fireweed in beach grasses on wetlands, Juneau
(opposite page) Salmonberries, Granite Creek Basin, Juneau

Ten-year-old anglers with a king salmon they caught on Admiralty Island.

Life on the Rainy Side

A hardy bunch, Southeasters. Whether catching air on a trampoline or trolling for salmon, we learn early on that you can't wait for sunshine to have some fun. Raincoats? Strictly optional.

Two boys and a dog prepare for a skiff ride from Funter Bay on Admiralty Island to Juneau.

(opposite page) All rain-geared up, two kids share a sopping wet trampoline jump in Funter Bay, Admiralty Island.

KETCHIKAN

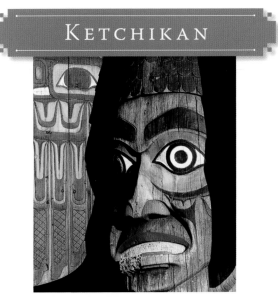

Ketchikan is the blue-collar soul of Southeast, and proud of it. Stretched along the shore of Revillagigedo Island, at the southern edge of the Inside Passage, this town of roughly 14,000 calls itself the gateway to Alaska—no idle boast a 100 years ago, and still true enough now. While the downtown waterfront is now occupied by jewelry and souvenir stores instead of a working sawmill's grubby sprawl, and in recent years has undergone a beautification program aimed at attracting summer visitors (900,000 by cruise ship alone), such a transformation isn't out of character. Riding out the waves of boom and bust, Ketchikan has reinvented itself several times and remains definitively Alaskan—individualistic, a little rough around the edges, rooted to its unique history, and to a heartfelt connection with the wild sweep of land and water that surrounds it.

(above) Detail from the "Wandering Raven House Entrance Pole",
Totem Bight State Historical Park, Ketchikan
(left) Creek Street at high tide, Ketchikan

Cruise ships at the dock in Ketchikan

KETCHIKAN

A visionary, enterprising Irishman named Mike Martin single-handedly willed modern Ketchikan into being. In 1885 Martin staked a claim at the mouth of Ketchikan Creek, the site of a Tlingit fish camp; five years later, he presided as mayor and king-pin over an incorporated town of 800 souls, carved into the steep flank of Deer Mountain and thrust out on boardwalks over tide-water. The new community included a salmon saltery, trading post, saloon, school, churches, and stairways designated as streets (some of which still exist today)—and most important of all, piers and services for a burgeoning flow of freight and passenger vessels headed north into the new territory of Alaska. Not all the boats carried fortune seekers. As early as the 1920s steamship tourism had become a well-established part of Ketchikan's economy.

Sunset over float plane dock,
Tongass Narrows, Ketchikan

So were prostitution, gambling, and bootlegging. Creek Street, a double row of buildings built on pilings along Ketchikan Creek, was for decades the center of riotous (but largely tolerated) vice. The district today is a picturesque collection of historic buildings where visitors stroll, shop, and watch salmon finning in the clear green water below.

Booms in salmon and mining came and went in Ketchikan; timber followed in the latter half of the 20th century, its decline spurred by a shift in global markets as well as widespread public opposition to large-scale clear-cutting of old-growth spruce and cedar. The Ketchikan Pulp Mill, at the time the town's leading employer, closed its doors in 1993. Today, timber plays a far smaller but vital economic role; commercial fishing and processing remains an important industry, as does the local shipyard, which is capable of handling large vessels. Ketchikan's role as a regional hub for transportation, shopping, and services contributes to a diversified, increasingly stable economy.

But there's little doubt that tourism drives the town that was once Mike Martin's private empire. Late May through early September, as many as 10,000 cruise visitors a day disembark, eager to shop, soak up the ambiance, and sample a variety of attractions, including a theatrical, pack-em-in lumberjack show, tours by air and boat to spectacular Misty Fiords National Monument, cable zipline rides through the rain forest canopy, and visits to Ketchikan's world-class totem parks. The cruise ships and Alaska Airlines jets come and go, and the channel in front of town buzzes with floatplanes—1,200 takeoffs or landings a day in peak season, enough to rank the local flight service station busiest in the nation for volume of radio traffic.

Fireweed and totem poles,
Totem Bight State Park, Ketchikan

Logger from Great Alaskan Lumberjack Show, Ketchikan

But underneath the carnival veneer, Ketchikan remains true to its roots. Stroll the waterfront along the industrial piers outside the tourist zone and you'll sense the same can-do, rough-knuckled spirit you would have found a century ago. And while folks are friendly as a rule across Southeast Alaska, Ketchikan may just set the regional standard—testament to a deep-rooted pride in who they are, their lifestyle, and this little rain forest town they call home. As Erin Jakubek, who's lived all of her 20-some years here says, "Ketchikan is a place where you don't have to be a millionaire to live on the water and eat king salmon and crab." She's got a pretty good point.

Float home, Ketchikan

Totem detail, Saxman Totem Park, Ketchikan

Totems

LOOMING OUT of the Pacific coastal mist, their origins shrouded in mystery, the totem poles of Southeast Alaska stand as testaments to the vigor and aesthetic brilliance of the Tlingit, Haida, and Tsimshian cultures. Carved of red cedar—clear-grained, easily worked, naturally resistant to decay—totem poles, historic to contemporary, have been created in a variety of styles and sizes. However, all poles are similar in one respect: they're monuments in the purest sense, reminders of a rich and ancient heritage. And, while just about every community in Southeast has its share, Ketchikan lays claim to the largest collection of totems in the world.

(left) Detail from the "Wandering Raven House Entrance Pole",
Totem Bight State Historical Park, Ketchikan

A carved eagle sits on top of totem pole in Saxman Totem Park, Ketchikan.

Though a pole can't be read or translated in some systematic way, its messages can be understood, both within context of the owner's clan and a larger cultural framework. As such, its carefully rendered figures are laden with meaning. These stylized forms may be animal, human, or mythical, and often represent heraldic clan crests. Some poles tell stories, while others commemorate events or stand as funerary monuments.

A live eagle sits on top of "The Pole on the Point" totem pole in Totem Bight State Historical Park, Ketchikan.

Clan house, Saxman Totem Park, Ketchikan

TOTEMS

The late 19th century marked the height of totem carving, but by the turn of the century, acculturation and unscrupulous collectors had taken their toll. However, a resurgence of cultural pride, a flurry of restoration projects, and the determination of a few master carvers proved victorious. By the 1960s a full-fledged revival was underway, one that continues to this day. Parks like Saxman and Totem Bight in Ketchikan, and Totem Park in Sitka attract throngs of visitors. Poles, both older and newly commissioned, stand before public buildings, businesses, schools, in museums, and—most important of all—in the communities where they were created. Totem pole carving, both traditional and purely artistic, continues to evolve. Like honored guests at a potlatch, they stand as witnesses to the celebration.

(opposite page) Celebrated master Tlingit carver, Nathan Jackson, works on a totem pole in the carving shed at Saxman Totem Park, Ketchikan.

A logger works a crosscut saw during the lumberjack show.

Logging

LOGGING WAS ONCE the region's lifeblood. For the first white settlers, the ancient rain forests were a ready and available resource, as they'd been, on a much smaller scale, for the Tlingit, Haida, and Tsimshian peoples who constructed houses, canoes, tools and artwork from the trees that surrounded them, and even wove cloth and braided rope from cedar bark. As the region grew, entire towns sprung from logs laboriously felled and milled by the blows of axes and the long crosscut saws known as "misery whips." Boats, barrels, piers, and boardwalks were shaped from sweat and sawdust.

Modern logging, mechanized and industrial in scale, remains what it always was — a physically demanding, perilous way of life, and a source of enormous pride to the men and women who've made it their own. Ketchikan's Great Alaskan Lumberjack Show celebrates and showcases the skills that built this land.

A lumberjack free-falls down a pole during the climbing competition.

(opposite page) Cast members of the Great Alaskan Lumberjack Show compete in the log rolling event.

New Eddystone Rock rises 237 feet above the waters of Behm Canal, Misty Fiords.

KETCHIKAN

Misty Fiords

MISTY FIORDS STANDS AS A TESTAMENT to the raw power of ice. Though the great tidewater glaciers that carved this remarkable national monument have now vanished, sculpted blue granite cliffs bear witness to their force. These features are showcased by the Punchbowl near the mouth of Rudyerd Arm—a 3,000-foot-high ice-age cathedral ground from living stone. But the scale of the surrounding landscape transcends any single vista. In the vertical realm of Misty Fiords, more than two million acres of salt-water passages, verdant forest, alpine lakes, and mountain-draped waterfalls, the spectacular becomes commonplace.

A float plane flies up Rudyerd Bay toward the cliffs in Punchbowl Cove, Misty Fiords National Monument.

Locals refer to this rock face towards the back end of Rudyerd Bay in Misty Fiords as "Owl Eyes" or "Owl Cliffs."

SITKA

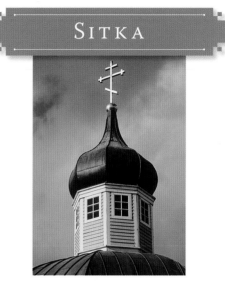

Sitka is simply gorgeous. Nestled into a protected anchorage on the outer coast of Baranof Island, this historic town lies in the midst of a land and seascape unlike any other. Alp-like spires rise behind town; to the west, the green waves of the open Pacific break against a scattering of reefs and small islands wrapped within the verdant arms of Sitka Sound. And against that wide seaward sky looms the volcanic cone of Mount Edgecumbe, bathed in banks of ocean mist. One has the impression that all the scenic elements were arranged as an enormous ornamental garden with the town at its center.

Sitka, however, offers more than just a pretty face. Twenty-four sites on the National Register of Historic Places, seven of which are designated as National Historic Landmarks, bespeak a rich and dramatic human past. For more than 50 centuries the Tlingit

(above) St. Michael's Catheral, Sitka
(left) A troller cruises through Sitka Sound with
the Rockwell Lighthouse in the distance.

City lights of Sitka from Harbor Mountain

reigned; the Kiksadi clan called their settlement Shee Atika. Ranging the coast in ocean-going cedar canoes, they drew on both the land and sea's bounty—resources that allowed them the leisure to develop elaborate works of art and a culture rich in formal ceremony.

In 1799 Russian fur traders arrived. Under the leadership of Alexander Baranov, they built a fort, and, with their Aleut slaves, slaughtered sea otters and seals for their pelts by the countless thousands. Some Tlingit welcomed the opportunity for trade; most considered the newcomers to be invaders. In 1802 a war party attacked the Russians, killing most and burning their stockade to the ground. The victory, though, was short-lived. Baranov returned in force two years later and after a naval bombardment, the Tlingit abandoned their defenses. The town of New Archangel was born. Within a matter of decades, it became the center for commerce and government in Russian America, complete with a cathedral, a number of two and three story buildings, a shipyard, sawmills, foundries, and an opulent governor's mansion. But shifting political fortunes in the wake of the Crimean War and the decline of the sea otter trade caused the Russians to lose interest in their colony, and they negotiated its sale to the United States. The ceremonial transfer of Alaska took place in Sitka on October 18, 1867, signaling a new era for both the town and the sprawling territory.

Fishermen work on their gear in Sitka.

Injured bald eagle in captivity at Sitka Raptor Center

SITKA

Fast forward to modern Sitka. While a 19th century Russian would of course marvel at the modern airport, the cars, and the cruise ships anchored offshore, he'd have little trouble recognizing the original Russian Bishop's House, St. Michael's Cathedral or the log blockhouse on Castle Hill (the latter two careful replicas). He would certainly not be overwhelmed by the current population level, which remains around 9,000. And the landscape, with its distinctive features, has changed little. The gold rushes at the turn of the century bypassed what was once dubbed "The Paris of the Pacific"; growth over the past hundred years has been, with the exception of the World War II era's boom, modest and steady. Industrial logging has come and gone; commercial fishing remains important. Many residents, including descendents of the Kiskadi Tlingit, rely on gathering from the land and sea, as they have for generations.

Totems in Sitka National Historical Park

Sunset behind Mt. Edgecumbe west of Sitka

As with Ketchikan, the visitor industry has clearly emerged as the driving force behind Sitka's economy. The town's rich past is by itself an attraction. A history buff can spend hours wandering the various architectural features, landmarks, and museums. The Sitka National Historical Park also encompasses the 1804 battleground and remains of the Kiskadi fort, in addition to an elegant totem park and cultural center. The popular Sitka Raptor Center, where injured birds are rehabilitated for release in the wild, offers the opportunity to get up-close to eagles and other birds of prey. Shopping the pleasant downtown area for Alaska crafts and souvenirs is another major draw. But Sitka Sound itself deserves top billing. Featured activities include truly world-class sport fishing, kayaking, and guided excursions to view sea life and the St. Lazaria National Wildlife Refuge. Sitka's timeless, radiant beauty ebbs and flows like ocean mist.

Soaring eagles, Sitka

Sitka Sound

SITKA SOUND VIBRATES WITH LIFE. In the lee of scattered islands, kelp forests sway in the tidal pulse; sea otters forage, and eagles soar overhead. Swirling shoals of capelin and herring nurture a myriad of sea creatures, including dozens of fish species, sea lions, seals, and humpback whales. The tracks of Sitka deer trace the tide lines, and great coastal brown bears patrol the creek mouths, feeding on sedges and spawning salmon.

Though life flourishes elsewhere in the more protected waters of the Inside Passage, here the feel is different. The rolling, insistent swells of the Pacific surge into the northward-curving funnel of the Sound, battering exposed shores where ancient drift logs lie in silver-gray skeins. The western horizon stretches huge, cloud-piled, and ever-shifting. Rising over Kruzof Island, the truncated, volcanic cone of Mount Edgecumbe reflects the luminous shades of sea and sky.

Tremendous sport fishing defines Sitka Sound. The catch rate for saltwater king salmon ranks the highest in the state, and charters working the outside coast return with huge hauls of halibut and ling cod. Opportunities for viewing marine life, especially sea otters, abound. These charismatic, sea-going members of the weasel clan, hunted into virtual extinction a century ago, have since recovered; rafts of grooming or resting otters are again a common sight.

Breaching humpback whale, Sitka Sound

Pigeon guillemots, St. Lazaria Island

Sea otters, Sitka Sound

Harbor seals, Sitka Sound

SITKA SOUND

Near the mouth of the Sound lies 65-acre Saint Lazaria Island, part of the Alaska Maritime National Wildlife Refuge. Set aside for protection since 1909 by President Theodore Roosevelt, its surreal lava features and sloping green uplands are home to millions of nesting sea birds of 21 species, including pelagic cormorants, pigeon guillemots, tufted puffins, and an estimated quarter million nesting pairs of storm-petrels. The latter two species dig extensive burrows that honeycomb the island. Here and elsewhere, tidal pools beckon, bright with life.

Exploring all the hidden inlets and islands of the Sound, knowing each kelp bed and reef intimately, would take a lifetime. But even a few hours here—time to inhale the sharp tang of salt air, trace the outline of a bear track on the beach, watch an otter mother cradling her pup—is enough to forge an unforgettable connection.

Visitors explore beaches on Kruzof Island, Sitka Sound.

(right) Rock formations on St Lazaria Island

Northern sun star

Constellations of Life

While humpback whales, seals, and sea otters may take center stage, the countless tidal pools scattered along the shores of Sitka Sound offer a glimpse into a no less spectacular world. A myriad of life forms glitter in delicate patterns as they move and breathe with the tides.

Thomas Jefferson Middle School Library
Decatur, IL

Purple sea star

Sea sponges at low tide on St Lazaria Island

(left) St. Lazaria Island National Wildlife Refuge and extinct volcano, Mt Edgecumbe

TRACY ARM

Tracy Arm: a rather ordinary name for an extraordinary place, arguably one of the most spectacular glacial fjords in both Alaska and the world—32 miles long and averaging a mile wide, surrounded by steep mountain walls rising up to 7,000 feet from sea level. Famed naturalist John Muir thought enough of Tracy Arm to proclaim that "no ice work I have ever seen surpasses this, either in the magnitude of the features or effectiveness of composition."

Tracy Arm is the northernmost of three narrow fjords—Tracy, Endicott, and Fords Terror—that together make up the Tracy Arm-Fords Terror Wilderness, about 45 miles southeast of Juneau. By virtue of its dramatic relief, Tracy stands without question above the others.

(above) Passengers photograph Sawyer Glacier, Tracy Arm.
(left) A ship cruises by icebergs in Tracy Arm.

TRACY ARM

Due to the rugged nature of the terrain, the only practical way to explore the area is via the deep, saltwater passages carved into this wilderness by the hands of ice. A matter of miles translates into centuries of change, traced by the succession of vegetation patterns. The world remains comparatively soft and green at the Arm's mouth, with broad patches of spruce and western hemlock. Inland 10 miles, past the "big bend"— a 90-degree turn in the fjord's course from north to east—evergreens diminish in frequency and size, and gradually give way to pioneering bands of birch, willow, and alder. Anchoring species such as lichens, fireweed, and sedges cling to toeholds in the rock.

Barren, striated granite walls increasingly predominate, and the journey ends at walls of ice: Sawyer and South Sawyer glaciers. Their dramatic, crevasse-riddled faces reign over the upper Arm, mysterious and ever-changing, sometimes shearing off in thunderous displays.

(left) The South Sawyer Glacier face dwarfs a catamaran in Tracy Arm.

The glacier front of South Sawyer Glacier, Tracy Arm

Mountain goats touch noses, Tracy Arm.

No Place Like Home

The near-vertical, barren rock walls and the tide-swept, frigid chaos of icebergs surrounding Tracy Arm's glaciers seem forbidding to human visitors. Yet they form ideal habitat to the creatures that make their homes in the shadow of ice.

Harbor seals rest on icebergs near South Sawyer Glacier.

(left) Steep fjord walls reflect in the ice-choked water of Tracy Arm.

Iceberg in Tracy Arm

TRACY ARM

The dynamic environment in the shadow of the glaciers creates a magnet for wildlife. Dozens, sometimes hundreds, of harbor seals haul out on the ice floes near South Sawyer Glacier, which provide safe haven for their young. Far up the Arm's ice-gouged walls, mountain goats traverse narrow ledges. Sea birds—including arctic terns, marbled murrelets, and pigeon guillemots—nest and feed near the face of the glaciers, where the nutrient-rich stirring of fresh and salt water provides abundant food. Though larger sea mammals such as humpback whales, killer whales, and Steller sea lions seldom range inside the Arm proper, they're commonly spied on the trip to or from Juneau.

In the end, a journey to Tracy Arm isn't about a checklist of creatures spotted, a collection of facts or figures, or an accounting of miles on a map. Surely such details add richness, but ultimate meaning lies in grasping the magnitude of what you've seen—the drama of creation and destruction that lies at the heart of all being, cast in a scale so grand it must be felt rather than understood. And fleeting images fill in the rest—skeins of mist draped across mountain shoulders, the sudden appearance of a seal's long-whiskered face at boatside, angled sunlight filtering through a blue iceberg. All are part of this timeless place, where change is the only constant.

(opposite page) Icy Falls, Tracy Arm

JUNEAU

Fᴿᴏᴍ ᴀ ᴠɪsɪᴛᴏʀ's ᴘᴏɪɴᴛ, Jᴜɴᴇᴀᴜ's ɢᴏᴛ ɪᴛ ᴀʟʟ—a chunky handful of glaciers draining a spectacular mountain-rimmed ice field, the best whale watching in the state, a postcard downtown lined with galleries, a gondola tram providing walk-on alpine access, fishing, river rafting, kayaking, flightseeing, and more, all within minutes of each other. Though every community in Southeast can claim its unique local attractions, for sheer variety in an accessible package, it's tough to beat the capital city.

While Juneau's a terrific place to visit, most residents agree it's an equally great place to live. Born and raised or transplanted, folks downright adore the place. An extensive network of hiking trails and public harbors leading into mountain and ocean wilderness, plus a quality municipal ski area, add up to an outdoor paradise.

(above) Governor's Mansion, Juneau
(left) Fireweed in full bloom in front of Mendenhall Glacier, Juneau

Brave boys take the plunge off Juneau's downtown cruise ship dock.

JUNEAU

Fine arts include a symphony orchestra, a classy state museum, professional theatrical productions, and a seemingly endless flow of festivals, exhibits, visiting artists, and lectures. A solid school system, libraries, clubs, activities and sports for all ages, a modest crime rate...across the board, Juneau qualifies as the eminently livable community *Outside Magazine* labeled it in 1993 (when it was ranked number five nationally).

So why isn't the population closer to a million instead of roughly 30,000? Well, there's that weather thing. Like every place in Southeast, rain's part of the deal—a 100 or so inches each year. And not all at once, but in foggy, soggy dribs and drabs, on and off for weeks at a time. Forty-some clear days annually is the average; five in a row practically amount to drought. Though winters aren't frigid by Alaska standards, conditions can verge on downright grim. One morning might be five below zero with three feet of snow on the ground; the next 35 above, with driving rain.

Isolation, and its attendant effect on the cost of living, add to the minus pile; the only way in or out is via the state ferry system, or one of a handful of daily jets heading north toward the main body of Alaska, or south toward Seattle. The single highway in town, known to locals as The Road, parallels the coast north to south for a total of 52 miles before dead-ending in gravel turnarounds. The steep terrain and convoluted shoreline dictate water and air as the paths of least resistance. Everything from fuel oil to fresh strawberries comes by long-distance barge or air freight—at a cost. Whatever else Juneau is, it ain't cheap.

View of downtown Juneau from Douglas Island

Bronze grizzly bear sculpture in downtown Juneau

Hawthorne flowers and totem pole next to the Juneau-Douglas Museum

JUNEAU

One positive effect of Juneau's relatively small size is a sense of familiar egalitarianism that hearkens to an earlier time. It's nothing to run into your senator or representative while you're walking your dog, greet him or her by name, and get a reply in kind. The wealthy and well-connected troll for salmon, shop, and stand in the same line at the post office with everyone else.

That sort of contact, along with being the epicenter of state government, make for an avidly, adamantly political town. Topics ranging from offshore oil lease sales to aerial wolf control inspire debate in supermarkets, at coffee stands, and on bumper stickers. Perhaps the single most longstanding and heated local discussion revolves around the future of that aforementioned Road. About half of all Juneauites clamor for it to be extended north to Skagway and union with the national grid. The remaining half stand bitterly opposed, convinced that such a link would doom all that makes Juneau itself. An industrial-scale gold mine at pristine Berners Bay, just beyond The Road's current endpoint, adds fuel to the controversy. Such debate stands emblematic of the larger, ongoing issue of developing the wild—how much, when, where—facing all Alaskans in the coming decades.

Despite the cost of living, weather, and isolation, Juneau continues to grow: from a few hundred miners and transient Tlingit in the late 1880s to 18,000 souls in 1980 to more than 30,000 in

Red Dog Saloon in downtown Juneau

2006. Parking lots, national franchise stores, and suburban developments steadily overtake the forest, moving ever higher up the mountains and farther out The Road.

Meanwhile, life goes on. Even at the height of summer, when some days land 10,000 visitors from five different cruise ships at once, on some nearby hiking trails you're almost as likely to meet an ambling black bear as a person. The fishing's still pretty darn good within sight of town, and for the hard-core adventurer, solitude echoes just an hour or two away. The landscape, once infinite, seems large enough. And Juneau, its adoring fans say, remains the same great town it always was.

Parasailer soars off Mt. Roberts above Juneau's Gastineau Channel.

A Tlingit tree carving along the trails on top of Mt. Roberts

Accessible Alpine

The Mount Roberts Tramway affords visitors and residents
alike a unique opportunity for easy access to alpine terrain
above the tree line. Rewards include eagle eye views of Juneau,
Gastineau Channel, and mountains rolling off to the horizon.
Marmots whistle from their burrow entrances, ptarmigan
chuckle, and bald eagles ride the updrafts.

Hoary marmot along trail

*(right) The Mt. Roberts Tram car carries visitors
up to the 1,800-foot level on Mt. Roberts.*

A humpback whale tail lifts clear of the water as it prepares to dive.

Wildlife Watching

You hear the whales as well as see them—*uurrhhh*, the huge sighing steam of their emptying lungs echoing off the green, mist-draped shoreline. Three humpbacks work across the bow in a slow-motion ballet, spouting and rolling in turn, and one by one lift flukes and dive.

Whale watching boat with a killer whale in view

While all the waters of Southeast offer opportunities to watch whales and other marine mammals, it's hard to match the dependable summer action in the Juneau area. Tails and spouts are common enough, but local humpbacks also engage in a cooperative feeding technique known as "bubble netting," where as many as a dozen whales use exhaled bubbles to corral baitfish, then lunge through the surface together, jaws agape. The tide-swirled channels around Juneau are also prime spots for patrolling orcas, sometimes in pods numbering 50 or more. Steller sea lions, declining elsewhere, are a sure bet; favorite sunning spots include local navigational bouys. Harbor and Dall's porpoises, seals, various seabirds, and eagles add variety. And on the right day, you may see them all.

Steller sea lions bask on a navigational buoy in front of Herbert Glacier, Juneau.

A sea gull narrowly misses the gaping mouth of a feeding humpback whale, Juneau.

With the Mendenhall Glacier in the background, a visitor strolls the path to the visitor's center.

Sockeye salmon in Steep Creek in the Mendenhall Glacier Recreation Area

Mendenhall Glacier

IF GLACIERS ENTERED BEAUTY PAGEANTS, the Mendenhall would take Miss Congeniality hands-down. Favored by travelers and locals alike, Juneau's neighborhood glacier is about as visitor-friendly as it gets. Concrete walkways lead to a number of vantage points, including a gorgeous visitor center with an indoor panoramic view of the glacier's mountain-rimmed lakeshore setting. Waterfalls plunge over gray, ice-gouged rock, and dense forests of spruce and hemlock tower into the mist. Miles of trails, from easy to increasingly challenging, radiate outward and upward. On the high slopes of Mount McGinnis and Mount Bullard, mountain goats graze, visible as off-white specks. Midsummer into autumn, spawning salmon attract black bears to nearby Steep Creek, where elevated boardwalks and platforms often afford close-up viewing just steps from the parking lot. Excursions in the glacier's shadow include river rafting, rides on the lake in a replica Tlingit war canoe, and helicopter shuttles accessing the magical world of the upper glacier, and the Juneau Ice Field beyond.

Rafting the Mendenhall River in front of the Mendenhall Glacier

Juneau Ice Field

Glacier trekkers explore crevasses on the "Hole in the Wall Glacier" in the Juneau Ice Field.

IMAGINE, IN A MATTER OF MINUTES, being whisked away from gravity, up into another world—a surreal, blue-white land where mile-high peaks are dwarfed by the sheer ache of space between them, and time itself seems frozen. Welcome to the Juneau Ice Field. This expanse of snow-laden ice and naked rock lies in a cradle of jagged peaks high in the Coast Mountains. Sprawling across the boundary between Alaska and British Columbia, it ranks as the fifth-largest ice field in all of North America; it feeds thousands of streams and dozens of rivers, including the great, sprawling Yukon, which will carry some of the Field's meltwater 2,000 meandering miles to the Bering Sea.

Thanks to its proximity to Juneau (a short ride by helicopter, including an exhilarating, ridge-hugging climb from sea level to several thousand feet) the Juneau Ice Field is among Alaska's most accessible, and local outfitters offer a range of guided activities including dog sledding, glacier treks, and aerial tours over this land of perpetual snow—the Alaska so many imagine.

This wide-flung landscape is a lens into eons past, the ice-age world some of our ancestors must have known intimately. Though still grand in scale, the Field is little more than a shrunken remnant of the vast, shifting sheets of ice that once lay over much of Southeast Alaska. The earliest archeological signs of human presence in the region date back 10,000 years, shortly after the onset of the current and most recent warming trend. Without this respite from the spell of ice, human habitation on any scale would have been impossible.

Jutting above the white, rolling face of the Field are knife-edged rock pinnacles known as nunataks (from the Yu'pik and Iñupiat Eskimo, "rock islands")—the protruding peaks of mountains submerged in enormous depths of ice. The summits of the tallest, the Snow Towers, exceed 7,000 feet. Their presence not only creates dramatic relief that increases the sense of scale, but provides islands where lichens, small plants, insects, and even mammals are able to maintain footholds.

(left) Helicopter over Juneau Ice Field

Glacier trekkers walk across the "Hole-in-the-Wall Glacier" in the Juneau Ice Field.

Summertime snowball fight on Mendenhall Glacier, Juneau Ice Field

JUNEAU ICE FIELD

Though it may appear motionless and permanent, the Juneau Ice Field is a dynamic, constantly shifting landform. Essentially a gigantic, frozen lake, it's fed by up to 100 feet of snow each year and drained by roughly three dozen "rivers"—the glaciers that rumble, grind, and slide down the valleys they've gouged from living rock, their daily progress measured in inches, occasionally feet. The equation of glacial flow, though affected by a number of variables, is essentially simple: if the volume of snowfall at a glacier's headwaters exceeds its rate of flow and annual rate of melting, it advances. If the snowfall (compressed by weight and time into ice) isn't sufficient and temperatures lower down are too great, the glacier retreats—melts faster than it moves downhill. Juneau's Mendenhall, like the vast majority of Alaska's glaciers, is losing ground; the Taku Glacier, just a few miles south and also a major outlet of the Ice Field, grinds steadily forward, its advance apparently due to its source being somewhat higher. The ebb and flow of ice, and the complex forces behind it, remain both spectacle and mystery.

Helicopter flies over a meltwater
pond on the Mendenhall Glacier.

A sled dog slaps an affectionate kiss on a grinning visiting musher.

Pack It In, Pack It Out

The three dog mushing camps on the Juneau Ice Field pose huge logistical issues. Everything and everyone—tents, sleds, hundreds of dogs, dozens of guides and handlers, food, fuel, and miscellaneous daily supplies, plus thousands of visitors—flies in and out via a seemingly endless procession of helicopters. Camps are completely removed at the end of each season and re-erected the following spring.

"If you're not the lead dog, the view is always the same."

(opposite page) This dog mushing camp on the upper reaches of the Mendenhall Glacier houses around 270 dogs.

Float planes tie up at Taku Glacier Lodge dock with East Twin Glacier in the background.

A Meal With A View

The historic Taku Glacier Lodge offers a quintessential Alaska experience—a fly-in salmon bake on the banks of the Taku River, with a full-front view of Hole-In-The-Wall Glacier. One of its former proprietors, Mary Joyce may be long gone, but tales of her exploits—including a 1,000-mile trip by dog sled to Fairbanks in the winter of 1935-36—is the stuff of local legend.

Trail marker sign

View of Taku Glacier Lodge along the Taku River

SKAGWAY

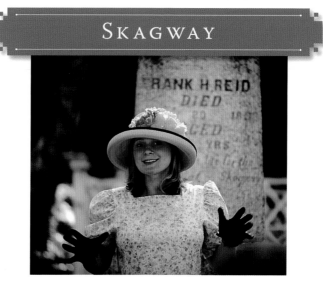

IF YOU LIKE YOUR ALASKA EXPERIENCE straight-up, Skagway's the place. Drop-dead photogenic, colorfully historic and conveniently compact, blessed with a sunnier climate than the rest of Southeast, this town of just 850 attracts nearly a 1,000,000 visitors a year—a staggering thousand-plus travelers for each local. Skagway's been described by both promoters and detractors as a gold-rush theme park. Either way, the Skagway faithful take exception to that label, which they feel short-changes their town.

When you stroll the boardwalks, down the row of frontier-quaint storefronts, you're walking in history's footsteps. Jewelry stores and souvenir kitsch may have made their inroads; however, most of the buildings, including the driftwood-emblazoned Arctic Brotherhood Hall, aren't movie-set props, but the real thing. They were standing in 1898 when Broadway was paved in ankle-deep

(above) A driver from the Skagway Street Car Company recounts a bit of the town's colorful history as she stands before Frank Reid's grave.
(left) A visitor walks past historic buildings along Broadway, the main street of Skagway.

mud, the gold rush hopeful by the tens of thousands shouldered through on their way to the fabled Klondike, and "Soapy" Smith's gang of cutthroats ruled the town, conning and murdering at will. Though Soapy and other colorful figures from the past live on in a long-running theatrical revue, they were all real enough. There on the outskirts of town lies Soapy's grave, and that of local hero Frank Reid, who fell mortally wounded after putting a bullet through the badman's heart.

Throughout the historic downtown district, from the Skagway Inn to the Red Onion Saloon and Moe's Frontier Bar, you can still practically hear the honkey-tonk piano, the whir of the roulette wheel, the occasional gunshot, and the laughter of ghosts. The National Park Service oversees much of the area, including portions of downtown, the nearby historic townsite of Dyea, and the Chilkoot Trail as a National Historic Park.

Spurred by headlines that screamed *Gold! Gold! Gold!*, over 100,000 men and women headed north by sail and steamship in 1898—a frenzied rush of epic proportions. Lying at points of access leading into the Canadian interior and the distant gold fields of the Klondike, the neighboring boomtowns of Skagway and Dyea sprang up. They mushroomed from disorganized clutters of tents and freight along the beaches to bustling, building-lined streets with breathtaking speed. While no exact census was possible, "Stroller" White, a popular wandering journalist of the period and one of Skagway's first tourists, reported a population between 8-10,000 in 1898. White also counted 70 saloons, and reckoned he'd missed a few. Dyea, two miles away, was almost equal in size. Each town touted its own route—Dyea's brutally steep but shorter Chilkoot Pass, and Skagway's more gradual White Pass, as the gateway to riches. By either route, the gold fields remained 600

A visitor pauses before the carefully restored Arctic Brotherhood Building, a unique Skagway landmark whose front includes more than 1,000 sticks of driftwood.

A sourdough with his husky poses for a photo amongst the flowers blooming along Broadway.

rugged miles distant. Fewer than half the would-be miners even completed the journey, and only a handful managed to both strike it rich and keep their fortunes (including a Seattle man named Nordstrom and a German guy who changed his name to Trump and invested in real estate.)

One of the mob on the Dyea beach was a green but optimistic young man, Jack London. Though he, like nearly all of his fellow adventurers, would find little in his gold pan, London retreated south after a winter in the Yukon with his fortune after all—scribbled journals and a headful of experiences from which he hewed *The Call of the Wild*, *White Fang*, and dozens of other tales. Canadian Poet Robert Service penned his celebrated collection of poems, *The Spell of the Yukon*, a decade after the rush of '98 had actually passed—while working as a bank clerk in Dawson City,

Yukon Territories. Both writers immortalized the heady, rough-and-tumble era, fixing it then and now in the public imagination.

The great Klondike gold rush ended as quickly as it had begun. Though Dyea withered and ultimately vanished, Skagway found renewed purpose. As the southern terminus of the narrow-gauge White Pass and Yukon Route Railway (started in 1898 and completed a decade later) it remained a vital link to the Canadian Yukon interior. And thanks to a combination of factors, not the least of which was the vision of writers like Service and London, Skagway became, even by 1900, what it remains today: a powerful magnet for travelers. Young and old alike, they come from all over the world to stroll up Broadway, lift their eyes to the wild mountains beyond, and—like so many before them—to dream.

The White Pass and Yukon Route Railway travels down the tracks just past mile 16 after Tunnel Mountain.

WP&YR

THE WHITE PASS AND YUKON ROUTE RAILWAY stands as one of the great rail engineering feats of all time. Climbing nearly 3,000 feet in its first 20 miles to the Summit of White Pass, negotiating cliff-hanging turns, bottomless canyons, and grades to nearly four percent, the narrow-gauge roadbed was quite literally carved into stone (including two tunnels through solid granite). Begun in April 1898, the bulk of the work was accomplished not by modern equipment but brute force—tens of thousands of men, countless horse and mule teams, and 450 tons of explosives. The weather during construction equaled the roughness of the terrain: periods of heavy rain, blanketing snows, and temperatures in one bitter stretch down to 60 below zero.

Envisioned to facilitate the movement of miners, supplies, and ore to and from the Yukon gold fields, the 110-mile project was completed in just over two years—too late for the rush itself, but on schedule for the less glamorous work that came later. Though industrial hauling comprised the railroad's bread and butter, the sheer, glacier-scoured terrain that had made the project so daunting soon proved an asset. Almost immediately after completion, the White Pass and Yukon gained popularity as a scenic excursion. The railroad now owes its very existence to the hundreds of thousands who each year travel the winding route to Summit Lake or beyond—a gravity-defying journey not only through space, but time itself.

White Pass & Yukon Route steam
engine #73 in downtown Skagway

The summit monument at mile 16.5 of the 33-mile Chilkoot Trail marks both the trail's high point at 3,246 feet and the border between the United States and Canada.

Skagway

Chilkoot Trail

THE CHILKOOT TRAIL IS A PERFECT MONUMENT to the great Klondike gold rush of 1898. This 33-mile overland route rising from tidewater at the ghost port of Dyea over the Chilkoot Pass was once a magnet for tens of thousands of fortune seekers. Endless, ant-like lines of them, backs bent under huge loads, toiled up the near-vertical "Golden Stairway" leading over the 3,246-foot Pass—a brutal yardstick measuring the limits of human ambition, endurance, and greed. A century later, the ribs of abandoned boats, rusting bits of metal, and undiscovered relics lie where they fell. The story of that time, a vein carved deep into the soil, seems no older than yesterday.

Historic relics dating from the late 1890s along the Chilkoot Trail

Hundreds of portable canvas canoes abandoned by gold stampeders lie scattered near the top of Chilkoot Pass.

GLACIER BAY

O F HIS 1880 VISIT TO GLACIER BAY, John Muir wrote, "When the sunshine is shifting through the midst of the multitude of the icebergs that fill the fjord and through the jets of radiant spray ever rising from the tremendous dashing and splashing of the falling and upspringing bergs, the effect is indescribably glorious." While the famed naturalist's rhapsodic prose might be a skosh over the top by modern standards, the intense beauty conveyed remains timeless. Muir's gushing accounts of the area were enough to fascinate the public. By 1900 more than 25,000 people had visited Glacier Bay on steamship pleasure cruises. More than a century later, the Bay remains what it was then: the premier wilderness destination in all of Southeast Alaska.

(above) A black oystercatcher in Dundas Bay, Glacier Bay National Park
(left) The three-hundred-foot face of Margerie Glacier in Glacier Bay National Park dwarfs a large cruise ship.

Humpback whale breaches in Glacier Bay National Park.

GLACIER BAY

This Yellowstone-sized national park and preserve includes 16 tidewater glaciers; several dozen alpine glaciers; a double-handful of dramatic fjords and inlets quite separate from Glacier Bay itself; the wild Alsek River; a stretch of surf-pummeled, seldom-visited outer coast; the great Brady Icefield; and portions of the rugged Chilkat and Fairweather mountain ranges.

Towering like an apparition over this god-sized landscape, the 15,320-foot prism of Mount Fairweather scrapes against the sky, refracting colors that have no earthly name. The mountain's vertical heave from sea level—an astounding 1,000 feet per linear mile—ranks among the most abrupt in the world. The Fairweather massif and its surrounding, somewhat lesser companions would be more than reason enough to justify a journey. Still, the centerpiece of Glacier Bay is what its name suggests: the spectacle of ice and its ancient work.

Johns Hopkins, Lamplugh, Reid, Muir, and McBride glaciers are all scenic and well known; but Margerie, in the northwest corner of Tarr Inlet, remains the most visited and photographed glacier in the park—and with good reason. Directly behind its furrowed, restlessly calving, blue-white brow looms arguably the most impressive backdrop for any glacier in Alaska: the gargantuan triple pyramids of Fairweather, 13,650-foot Mount Adams, and 12,000-foot Mount Salisbury. Due to the water depth against Margerie's mile long, 300-foot-high outer edge, vessels can pull practically alongside for spectacular viewing—and even mega-cruise ships are dwarfed in the process.

A few hundred yards to the north, almost touching Margerie and trailing off into Canada, lies the much lower, nearly land-stranded face of Grand Pacific Glacier, black with moraine debris. Two centuries earlier, this was the Mississippi of Glacier Bay's rivers of ice. The collective outpouring of it and its tributaries clogged the very mouth of the Bay itself, 70 miles away, where in 1794 Captain George Vancouver reported, "compact and solid mountains of ice" that towered a half mile. By the time of Muir's first visit in 1879, almost a hundred years later, the glacial front dominated by Grand Pacific had already receded 40 miles; the 20th century subtracted another 30. The documented retreat of ice in Glacier Bay has been the most rapid anywhere in the world—more than can be explained by the current global warming trend. Scientific interest in this phenomenal rate of change led to the Bay's initial protection in 1925 as a national monument and massive outdoor laboratory. Study continues to this day—not only of the factors involved (among them, earthquakes, under-ice water and thermal activity that speed up glacial flow and fragmentation) but of the land as it re-emerges from slumber under a centuries-old blanket of ice.

(opposite page) Grounded icebergs at low tide dwarf the photographer in front of Reid Glacier, Glacier Bay National Park.

A black bear eats spring sedges in Glacier Bay National Park.

GLACIER BAY

In the retreating shadow of the glaciers, life blossoms with almost startling rapidity. Cottonwood and spruce trees sprout where ice reigned just a decade before. Pink salmon and Dolly Varden char spawn in newly emerged streams. Marine and land mammals, including humpback whales, mountain goats, harbor seals, brown bears, and Steller's sea lions continue to expand their range up-bay. Shrimp-like krill bloom in the brackish turbulence along glacier faces, feeding colonies of gulls, terns, and kittiwakes. As the tide of ice recedes, the land burns green—as it has before, and will again.

Mountain goats rest in the shade on Gloomy Knob in Glacier Bay National Park.

Black-legged kittiwakes nest along the steep fjord walls near glacier faces in Glacier Bay National Park.

(opposite page) Sea lions in Glacier Bay National Park

The blue-white 300-foot-high Margerie Glacier face stands in stark contrast to the black, rubbled-covered face of Grand Pacific Glacier in Glacier Bay National Park.

(left) Ice chunks calve from the face of Margerie Glacier in Glacier Bay National Park.

Tlingit dancers from the village of Hoonah

Hoonah

HOONAH—the name echoes an ancient past. This community of 850 on remote Chichagof Island offers a glimpse into small-town Southeast Alaska that's bypassed by most travelers. Here, commercial logging and fishing blend with a proud Tlingit tradition. People don't just dance in their regalia for visitors; they do it for themselves. Icy Strait Point, a recently renovated, historic cannery, provides a waypoint for a limited number cruise ships each season. Guests can choose between taking a guided rain forest walk where bears are commonly sighted, shopping for local crafts, fishing, wildlife viewing, and more. Across Icy Strait, 22 miles to the northwest lies Glacier Bay—according to tradition, the ancestral homeland from which the Hoonah people were forced out of by advancing glaciers centuries ago. Today, the Eagle and Raven clans continue to live in two worlds: the rich and timeless past of their ancestors, and the onrushing, jet-age future. With one foot firmly in each, they dance.

A cruise ship anchors off the restored historic cannery in Hoonah.

The historic cannery building, Hoonah

GULF OF ALASKA

Seal lions bask on the rocks of Grotto Island in the Kenai Fjords National Park.

ROCKY COASTLINE ALONG THE GULF OF ALASKA, KENAI FJORDS NATIONAL PARK

GULF OF ALASKA

THE GULF OF ALASKA COAST includes some of the most remote and hauntingly beautiful wilderness in the state—or anywhere, for that matter. Along this sweeping 850-mile curve from Cape Spencer to the Kodiak Archipelago, settlements are few and the scale of land and sea equally enormous, featuring the highest coastal mountains in the world and the largest glaciers outside of Antarctica and Greenland. Here the surreal white battlements of the Fairweather, St. Elias, and Chugach ranges, crowned by 19,550-foot Mount Logan and 18,008-foot Mount Saint Elias, face off against the North Pacific's towering weather—waves of storms crashing islands, interspersed with huge, multilayered skies and flashes of brilliant blue. Glaciers drape down high valleys and flow seaward; dense forests of spruce and hemlock interspersed with marshy muskeg cloak the lowlands. Along mile after mile of surf-battered coast, human tracks are few.

The southernmost hundred miles includes the wild stretch of Glacier Bay National Park and Preserve known simply as the Outer Coast. Dominated by the backdrop of the Fairweather Range, it's cut by a half-dozen bays and fjords, including the equally notorious and gorgeous Lituya Bay. Over the past two centuries, at least 100 people have died at its tide-ripped entrance, including 21 of French explorer Jean La Perouse's men in 1786. Lituya is also the site of the highest ocean wave ever witnessed—a terrifying 1,720-foot monster set off by an earthquake-caused landslide in 1958. Geologically speaking, this was by no means an isolated

(preceding pages 99-100) View of glaciers along College Fiord in Prince William Sound

ALASKA

map area

ALASKA RANGE

CHUGACH MOUNTAINS

CANADA

Cook Inlet

○ **Anchorage**

Whittier ○ ○ **Valdez**

Prince William Sound

Homer ○ ○ **Cordova**

KENAI FJORDS NATIONAL PARK

○ **Seward**

WRANGELL-ST. ELIAS NATIONAL PARK

Hubbard Glacier

Gulf of Alaska

○ **Kodiak**

Yakutat ○

PACIFIC OCEAN

0   30   90   150 miles

N

GULF OF ALASKA

incident; scars of dramatic upheavals and subsidence are common throughout the region.

The northern extreme of the Glacier Bay parklands is bounded by the glacier-fed Alsek River. Popular with river-rafting adventurers, the Alsek cuts a dramatic, mountain-rimmed path from its headwaters in the Yukon Territories, across a slice of British Columbia to the Alaska coast at Dry Bay. And as far as the Gulf Coast goes, that's just a start. Ahead lies that unbroken panorama of mountains, glaciers, sea, and sky, stretching all the way through the wonders of Prince William Sound, and the ice-sculpted fjords and craggy headlands of Kenai Fjords National Park.

(left) The exotic geological formations in the Kenai Fjords National Park known as Spires Cove

An aerial view of Hubbard Glacier looking across its face toward Turner Glacier, from above Russell Fjord

Hubbard Glacier

Hubbard Glacier in Wrangell-St Elias National Park.

DYNAMIC AND RESTLESS, the Hubbard Glacier ranks among Alaska's most spectacular. In addition to being North America's longest tidewater glacier, over 90 miles from source to terminus, it's unique in one other respect. Over the past century, the Hubbard has been thickening and advancing. Great length relative to its calving front, acting in concert with other factors, seems to make it almost immune to climate change. In 1986 and again in 2002, Hubbard's advancing ice front dammed the mouth of 35-mile-long Russell Fjord, creating a rapidly rising lake. Both times the dam failed in an explosive cascade (a phenomenon known to glaciologists as a *jokulhlaup*) but not before threatening to engulf the entire Siktuk River system, a major sport-fishing resource and salmon spawning drainage vital to the town of Yakutat's economy. Watching scientists predict another damming event is likely, and the question of how to respond remains open. Meanwhile, visitors have a ringside seat to an unfolding geological drama of epic proportions.

PRINCE WILLIAM SOUND

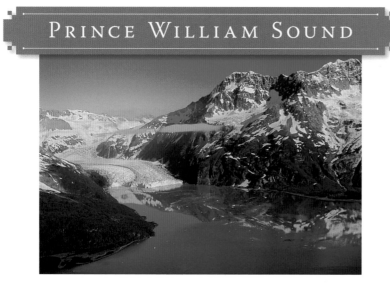

There's no place quite like Prince William Sound. Tucked into the eastern lee of the Kenai Peninsula and shielded from the Gulf of Alaska's tumult by a constellation of islands, the Sound, with its 3,000 miles of fjord-cut shoreline and ice-scoured depths, comprises a world of its own. Intimate as well as protected, latticed with hidden bays and coves, the scenery nonetheless stacks up large. Jagged peaks of the Chugach Range rise from water's edge. Vertical relief of 4 to 6,000 feet is the norm, and glaciers are commonplace—clinging to high cirques and benches, caught in frozen cascades down sheer slopes, rumbling and groaning seaward.

Prince William Sound enfolds 20 tidewater glaciers in all, the highest concentration on the planet. The western wall and head of twin-lobed College Fiord is lined with no fewer than six of

(above) Aerial view of Surprise Glacier in Prince William Sound
(right) Harbor seals on iceberg in front of Surprise Glacier in Prince William Sound

these within a panoramic, dozen-mile stretch. If names like Harvard, Yale, Vassar, and Bryn Mawr seem a bit incongruous given the setting, at least they're consistent. These appellations and others were bestowed, in somewhat colonial fashion, by members of the 1899 Harriman Alaska Expedition. The Sound, like much of Alaska, is a patchwork of labels bestowed by the latest passers-through. But in essence, the land remains as nameless as it always was.

Pristine as it may seem, parts of Prince William Sound remain profoundly affected by the catastrophic Exxon Valdez oil spill of 1989. Seven hundred miles of the Sound's shoreline were oiled, 200 of them severely. A quarter million sea birds and nearly 3,000 sea otters tallied among the almost incalculable losses; of the 26 species of birds, fish, and mammals that suffered "significant" damage, only two (bald eagles and river otters) have recovered fully; some, like the Sound's still-declining harbor seals and killer whales, may never. On some beaches, a thick layer of sludge remains a shovelful beneath the surface.

Though the total impact of this disaster remains staggering, all the news is by no means bleak. Nearly 760,000 acres of land in the Sound, much of it slated for logging, was purchased or protected with the $900 million paid in civil damages. Research and protection against future spills remain well funded. Nonetheless, Exxon, thanks to court maneuvering, hasn't paid a cent of the $5 billion levied in criminal penalties more than a dozen years ago.

Meanwhile, the Sound has quietly, almost miraculously, continued to heal itself. Its deep, cold waters teem with life, and clouds of sea birds again veer overhead. Otters and whales dive and feed; waterfalls gush down green hillsides, and the glaciers glow blue in the mist. Through all our wrangling, Prince William Sound abides.

(left) Fog, low clouds and rain shrouds the Cascade and Barry Glaciers in Prince William Sound.

Alaska Railroad cars near the cruise ship dock in Whittier

Backdropped by mountains around 3,000 feet high, Whittier spreads out along the shore of Passage Canal in Prince William Sound.

Whittier

Most of Whittier's residents live in the Begich Towers.

IMAGINE A COMMUNITY where most of the residents live in a single 14-story building, bears hibernate in an abandoned neighboring high-rise, and the connection to the outside world is a tunnel with a curfew. Welcome to Whittier, The Strangest Little Town in Alaska. Wedged into the head of a narrow, mountain-rimmed inlet, Whittier came into being as a secret military base in World War II—a strategically located, cloud-draped, ice-free port almost impossible to spot from the air. Though the base shut down in 1960, the town marches on, populated by roughly 200 year-round "Whidiots" (as some residents good-humoredly call themselves) and an equal number of "Half-Whits" who move in for the busy summer. The post-Stalin flavored, concrete architecture is hardly a draw, but the location is: the doorstep of Prince William Sound, one of Alaska's natural scenic gems.

SEWARD

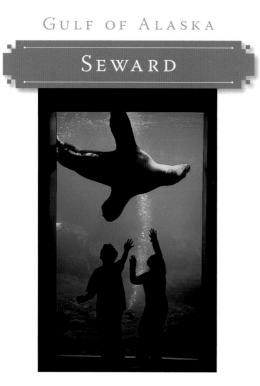

RESURRECTION BAY MAY BE the most aptly named geologic feature in all Alaska. A visitor strolling the waterfront of Seward, nestled at the bay's head, would find it hard to believe that just over four decades ago, this thriving, mountain-rimmed community was almost wiped off the face of the earth. On Good Friday, 1964, the great Alaska earthquake struck. Measuring 9.2 in magnitude, the quake, one of the most violent ever recorded, pummeled Southcentral Alaska. For five terrifying minutes, a series of bedrock-shifting temblors ripped gaping holes in the fabric of the land and in people's lives. Seward, along with a handful of coastal towns clustered near the epicenter, was the most severely hit.

(above) Children interact with a female sea lion at the SeaLife Center in Seward.
(right) An Alaska Railroad train crosses the Upper Trail Lake bridge near Moose Pass on its way to Seward.

A Seward dock dog carries a stuffed toy salmon up the ramp.

Sport fishing halibut harvest in Seward

SEWARD

Though the quake wrought fearsome damage—scars marking abrupt upheavals and drops still are visible today—the tsunamis that followed proved the real killers. Across the region, walls of water up to 200 feet high slammed into the dazed survivors, hurling boats, docks, railroad cars, buildings, and bodies into a tangled mass of wreckage. Seward's waterfront, like that of its sister cities Whittier and Valdez, was virtually obliterated; partially constructed on unstable fill, it collapsed into the harbor, triggering a local secondary tsunami of its own. Ruptured fuel tanks completed the hellish scene as their contents ignited, setting the water itself ablaze. In the final reckoning, 115 Alaskans died in these killer waves, including a dozen Seward residents.

Today, few hints of the carnage remain. The small boat harbor and downtown streets bustle with activity. Prosperous residential areas radiate outward and up verdant hillsides, beyond the reach of another tsunami. Seward ranks as one of the top 25 commercial fishing ports in the U.S., and, as southern terminus of the Alaska railroad, has developed into a significant shipping point for Asia-bound coal. And thanks to an unbeatable combination

Large sections of Seward's waterfront slid into the ocean during the Good Friday Earthquake in 1964. Now, most residences are built on higher ground, while the waterfront is set aside for parks and RV parking.

of scenic attributes, nearby recreational possibilities, and location (about four hours by rail and under three hours by road from Anchorage) Seward has continued to blossom as an accessible ocean playground for Alaskans and visitors alike.

Every afternoon, crowds gather at the docks to gawk at seemingly endless cartloads of halibut, salmon, rockfish, and ling cod brought in by the sport fishing fleet. The action reaches such unbelievable levels that anglers, some of them novices, can be heard fretting as they pose with their catch that their biggest halibut was "only" 70 pounds.

The Alaska SeaLife Center—both a world-class aquarium and a research facility with habitats featuring local marine life—attracts throngs of visitors; and no trip to Seward would be complete without a trip to Exit Glacier, a unique walk-up, self-guided experience just a 15-minute drive from downtown. Without question, the ocean wilderness of Kenai Fjords National Park stands high on Alaska's list of must-go experiences. But perhaps the largest attraction in Resurrection Bay remains the miracle of Seward itself: the town that the sea took away, and has since brought back.

A common murre in the sea bird habitat at the SeaLife Center

Alaska SeaLife Center

Seward's Alaska SeaLife Center stands out as one of the precious few good things to come from the Exxon Valdez oil spill. This beautifully designed, spacious facility features huge, view-from-above or below habitats where visitors can observe a myriad of species including juvenile harbor seals, puffins, and an enormous bull sea lion named Woody swimming quite literally eye-to-eye.

Its construction funded by oil spill settlement money, the SeaLife Center is far more than just a snazzy aquarium. Its four-tiered mission statement—research, rehabilitation, education and conservation—is addressed each and every day, furthering scientific knowledge, rescue of foundling or wounded animals, and public appreciation of the complex ecosystems and life forms of the Alaska Gulf Coast. And where else can you watch puffins flapping their wings as they swim underwater?

(opposite page) A young boy goes face to face with Woody, a 9½-foot-long sea lion weighing more than one ton, at the SeaLife Center.

A SeaLife staff member enjoys the company of an adult and an immature tufted puffin.

For The Birds

The Alaska SeaLife Center's bird habitat offers visitors a rare opportunity. Though most of the sea birds housed there can be easily seen in the wild, they're generally small and fast-moving, so often difficult to observe. At the Center's large, split-level habitat, viewers can watch and photograph a number of species up close, above and below the water, including everyone's hands-down favorite, puffins.

(opposite page) Tufted puffins couple in the sea bird habitat at the SeaLife Center.

Visitors hike on trails next to Exit Glacier in Kenai Fjords National Park, Seward.

Exit Glacier

COUNT ALL THE GLACIERS in Alaska, and hours or days later, you'd have a list scrolling off into the thousands. Now tally the number you could walk right up to, ten minutes from a parking lot. That list stacks up much shorter—exactly two, in fact: the Worthington Glacier near Valdez, and Exit Glacier, fed by the 300-square mile Harding Ice Field. Though far from the largest or most dramatic of Alaska's ice rivers, Exit remains the most accessible on the continent, a family-friendly attraction where anyone, from casual sightseer to mountaineer, will feel at home.

(opposite page) Ice face of Exit Glacier
in Kenai Fjords National Park

KENAI FJORDS

Kenai Fjords National Park is the sort of landscape that defines Alaska—a wilderness of glaciers, sculpted granite pinnacles, snowy peaks and deeply incised fjords. Easily accessible from nearby Seward, this 100-mile stretch of coastline, like most of the Gulf Coast, remains intensely wild and pristine. And though thousands of visitors a day pass through on tour boats, the vastness of Kenai Fjords—a labyrinth of passages, islands, and inlets—absorbs them all.

Offshore, sprawling out to the open North Pacific, lies the real wilderness: the turbulent Gulf of Alaska, some of the roughest and most unpredictable waters on the planet. By comparison, the enormity of the Kenai Fjords seems intimate. The restless pulse of swells surges against the outer islands and exposed headlands of the park, defining the edge of another world.

(above) Passengers on one of the many day boats visiting
Kenai Fjords National Park view the Aialik Glacier.
(left) Northwestern Glacier in Kenai Fjords National Park

KENAI FJORDS

At the mixing point between these two realms, where the comparatively shallow, saltier water of the Gulf meets the tide-swirled currents of fresh melt-water flowing off the land, life flourishes in almost startling profusion. Blooms of plankton and the small fish that feed on them set the food chain in motion. Salmon slash into balls of bait, flashing silver as they break the surface. Predatory marine mammals, including Dall's porpoise and harbor seals, find the hunting good, too. Steller's sea lions haul out on sloping granite ledges to bask; sea otters, floating on their backs, nap and groom. Showing flukes as they dive, humpback whales work the edges of tidal currents. Occasionally, the triangular fins of killer whales cut the water.

The sheer quantity and variety of bird life sets apart Kenai Fjords from other coastal areas. Tremendous colonies of sea birds, including kittiwakes, cormorants, gulls, murres, and puffins, nest on the spectacular granite outcroppings and ledges that are common in the park. Clouds of kittiwakes erupt from their nests, wheeling and calling whenever a bald eagle soars too close—a massive display known to biologists as a "dread flight." Feeding birds often dot the water in massive flocks that bespeak the even greater volume of life beneath the surface. In Kenai Fjords, the air and water are seldom still.

Sea otter, Kenai Fjords

(left) Kenai Fjords National Park showcases a variety of striking geological formations, including Grotto Island.

THE RAILBELT

BULL CARIBOU, ALASKA RANGE AND DENALI NATIONAL PARK

THE RAILBELT

THE VAST MAJORITY of Alaska's 600,000-plus residents live within a few miles of a railroad line. The Railbelt, as Alaskans call it, traces a 400-mile-long, north-south corridor stretching from Seward and Whittier on the southcentral coast through the Chugach Mountains to Anchorage, across the Matanuska and Susitna River valleys, past Denali National Park to Fairbanks. While not a region in the traditional sense of the word, the Railbelt nonetheless accurately describes Alaska's core of population and development, both historic and modern. Pioneers and prospectors traveling by horse, riverboat, on foot or by dog sled followed the same basic route, as do today's modern highways. The farmlands near Palmer, the major southcentral and interior coal fields, and the gold mining country near Fairbanks all lie near the route of the Alaska Railroad. And beyond that narrow band, just

over 600 miles of track, all told—the Great Land stretches away to a limitless horizon, scarcely marked by human progress.

Construction of the railroad began in 1903 as a private venture reaching north from the ice-free port of Seward. After four years and 50 miles, the Alaska Central Railway went bankrupt. In 1914 the federal government authorized funding to extend the railroad to Fairbanks. Total cost was estimated at $35 million, a staggering sum at the time. At its peak, the project employed 4,500 workers, many of whom labored 12-hour shifts under abysmal conditions—mosquitoes, mud, subzero cold, torrential rains—for a dollar a day. In 1923 President Warren G. Harding traveled north to drive a golden stake at Nenana, symbolizing the project's completion. By dark coincidence, this ceremonial act led to

(preceding pages 126-127) Evening falls over Mt McKinley/Denali and the Alaska Range in Denali National Park.

An Alaska Railroad train crosses the 914-foot-long, 296-foot-high Hurricane Gulch Bridge on its way south from Denali National Park to Anchorage.

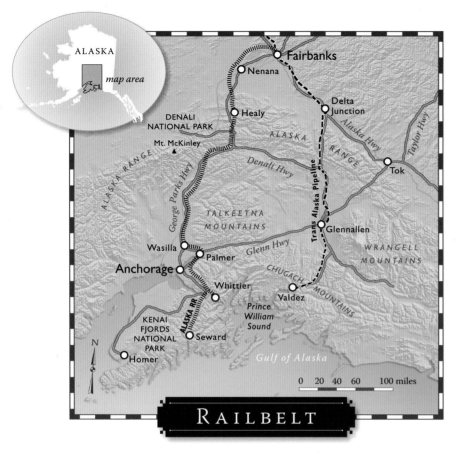

ALASKA

map area

Fairbanks

Nenana

Delta
Junction

Healy

DENALI
NATIONAL PARK

ALASKA

Mt. McKinley

Denali Hwy

Tok

TALKEETNA
MOUNTAINS

Glennallen

WRANGELL
MOUNTAINS

Wasilla

Palmer

Glenn Hwy

Anchorage

CHUGACH

Whittier

Valdez

Prince
William
Sound

KENAI
FJORDS
NATIONAL
PARK

Seward

N

Homer

Gulf of Alaska

0 20 40 60   100 miles

RAILBELT

Harding's death; on his return trip he died in San Francisco, a
victim of food poisoning.

Today, the Alaska Railroad is a state-owned, for-profit corporation—
the only full-service railroad (carrying both passengers and freight)
in the entire United States. While it's expanded very little since its
completion in terms of track miles, the quality of the infrastructure
continues to improve, from more powerful, fuel-efficient engines
and luxury cars with skylights to a just-completed terminal serv-
ing Anchorage's international airport. And thanks to its expanding
role in the visitor industry, the railroad continues to thrive. Roughly a half million passengers each year enjoy Alaska's scenic riches
as they travel from the cruise ship ports of Whittier and Seward to
Anchorage and a return flight home, or on to Denali National Park
and Fairbanks, in the heart of Alaska's Interior.

Trans Alaska Pipeline,
north of Fairbanks

ANCHORAGE

LOOKING OUT OVER THE SPRAWL of Anchorage, it's odd to think that Alaska's largest city started off as a construction camp. The current population—somewhere in excess of 260,000 within city limits, and at least a third more beyond—belies the significance of this pocket-sized metropolis. Located near the invisible cross-roads of the "great circle" air route connecting Europe, North America, and Asia, Anchorage's international airport stands as the planet's largest way station for air cargo, and a vital stopover for passenger jets. The local Federal Express complex is the cor-poration's largest facility anywhere.

(above) Float planes docked at Lake Hood. Alaska has six times as many pilots and 14 times as many aircraft per capita as the rest of the United States. One in every 65 Alaskans is a pilot.
(left) With the Chugach Mountains as a backdrop, the Anchorage skyline reflects in the waters of Cook Inlet at high tide.

Fishermen, Ship Creek, Anchorage

ANCHORAGE

Anchorage has cemented its role as Alaska's own transportation hub as well. Massive dockyard facilities for offloading container ships, most of the state's highway system, and the central railroad line converge there. And, in a land where people fly as a matter of course, most air routes, either to the Bush or to the outside world, lead through Anchorage, too. Where transportation leads, commerce follows. The city has morphed into the corporate headquarters for the major players in the state, from big oil to federal agencies to powerful Native corporations. Not to mention Los Anchorage (as some call it, with a mixture of disdain and grudging awe) reigns as the shopping mall for the entire state. To gauge the raw commercial clout of this town, consider that Costco's single highest-selling warehouse in their entire international chain is in…you guessed it.

With urban Anchorage in the background, anglers fish for salmon in Ship Creek.

The key to Anchorage's past, like its present, could be summed up by the old real estate adage, location, location, location. Given 20/20 hindsight and a decent eye for maps, anyone could have predicted the location of Alaska's central city. In 1914, engineers scouting the Alaska railroad's route found a handful of homesteaders near the mouth of Ship Creek, the best and farthest north anchorage for larger boats offloading freight (thus the name). A few months later, a tent city of more than 2,000 had sprung up, lured by rumors of employment on the rail project, which indeed proceeded almost straight north and south from the nascent camp, bisecting the territory. The need for order soon became self-evident. Streets, water and phone lines, electricity, schools, and the town's first concrete sidewalks followed within two years, along with a theater, an ice cream parlor, legal offices, and clothing stores. The railroad camp that woke up as a town never looked back. Explosive growth during World War II and the oil boom of the 1970s pulsed straight through town. Room for expansion and a moderate climate sealed the deal. After passing over the threshold of a new millennium, Anchorage continues to defy expectations. The question isn't if the city will continue to grow, but how much and how fast.

Anchorage is just a couple hours away from Alaska—there's more truth than ever in that old joke. But though the suburban mall sprawl continues its inexorable march outward, the wild filters through. Moose and bears amble daily through suburban neighborhoods; fishermen cast for (and catch!) big king salmon under a highway overpass near an industrial park. And the saw-toothed front of the Chugach Mountains still rises over the Anchorage bowl, as it has for millennia. In the shadow of fast-food restaurants and big-box stores, Alaska is still Alaska, after all.

DENALI NATIONAL PARK

THE MOUNTAIN, Alaskans call it. Or Denali—the High One. Rising from the heartland of Alaska's vast Interior, visible from hundreds of miles away, the blue-white bulk of Mount McKinley (as it's officially known) dominates both the horizon and our collective imagination. By any name, this four-mile-high pyramid of rock and ice looms as a symbol of all that is Alaska.

Fitting that The Mountain should be the centerpiece of the state's most visited and celebrated wildland, Denali National Park and Preserve. Two hundred forty miles north of Anchorage and 120 south of Fairbanks, the park totals six million acres—almost twice the size of Connecticut. This enormous area gathers in a double handful of varied terrain: birch and aspen-clad uplands; barren, saw-toothed ridges; bands of white and black spruce taiga; and deep within the park's highlands, the 20,320-foot

(above) Close-up view of Mt. McKinley/Denali in evening light
(right) Mt. McKinley/Denali mirrored in Reflection Pond, Denali National Park

Dall sheep ram, Denali National Park

DENALI NATIONAL PARK

Mount McKinley massif towering over the Alaska Range. Through the core of the park, open sweeps of sub-arctic tundra roll to mountain backdrops, a stage across which caribou, wolves, and grizzlies roam. A scenic 89-mile gravel road winds into the park's interior, offering visitors passage into this world where time seems to have scarcely begun.

Given that build-up, the mode of travel seems a bit incongruous. Concessionaire-operated buses reminiscent of high school days, leaving every few minutes, are the only traffic allowed past the Savage River, 15 miles into the park. Led by the driver, who doubles as guide, wildlife spotting and viewing becomes a cooperative exercise. Adventurous visitors have the opportunity to get dropped off by a bus at a given point (excluding some restricted areas) and picked up by the next bus traveling in either direction.

Guests of the park hope to at least glimpse two things: The Mountain, of course, and animals—preferably the aforementioned grizzlies, wolves, and caribou—in more or less that order. Heck, throw in a bull moose, a fox, or wolverine for good measure. And why not aim for the ultimate? But, if you allow personal fulfillment to hinge on these twin grails, be prepared for disappointment. The Mountain's fickleness is legendary, especially in summer. Piling up currents of wet air riding in from the Gulf of Alaska, it cycles through violent storm systems that often obscure its bulk. Veteran mountaineers wait for days, even weeks for clear climbing weather (the same that allows you to see The Mountain) and are often thwarted.

A Dall ram stands on a precipitous ledge in the high country of Denali National Park.

A herd of Dall sheep lambs and ewes rests in Denali National Park.

A visitor to Denali National Park
tries on a set of caribou antlers at
the Toklat Visitor's Center.

DENALI NATIONAL PARK

The wildlife is no more predictable. Keep in mind the old guide's adage: there's fewer animals out there than you think, and far more than you see. Eager travelers may be blessed enough to watch a female grizzly and cubs meander up the road, a pack of wolves feed on a moose kill, and a band of caribou graze close by, all in a matter of hours. Or they may hit a day where, inexplicably, nothing seems to be moving beyond an occasional marmot, some yellow-white specks that the driver identifies as Dall sheep, and some swaying alders where a moose's hind end disappeared. Nature, inside an iconic national park or not, answers to no one's bidding.

Should you go? Of course you should. Not in spite of, but precisely because of that uncertainty. Isn't that the whole point of Alaska, after all? Newcomer or lifelong Alaskan, we all come here to rediscover our place, small beneath the sky. The High One does loom into sight, lit with alpenglow, miraculously reflected in Wonder Lake. Grizzlies and wolves and caribou do roam that limitless tundra of possibility. Sit and watch and hope, and think about where you are.

Bull caribou in velvet in Denali National Park

Cow moose, Denali National Park

Red fox, Denali National Park

Willow ptarmigan, Denali National Park

Think Small

No one comes to Denali National Park hoping to see foxes, ground squirrels, or short-tailed weasels. But don't overlook the smaller creatures that form the fabric of this landscape. Their struggles for survival are no less dramatic than those of moose and wolves, and besides, it's hard to beat a pika (a palm-sized, rabbit-like rodent common in rocky areas throughout the park) for sheer charisma!

Ground squirrel, Denali National Park

Pika, Denali National Park

A grizzly bear mother and two cubs stroll along a piece of the 89-mile-long Denali Park Road.

Heart and Soul

If not for the road, a winding, 89-mile-long gravel track leading all the way to Kantishna, few of us would be able to access the splendor of Denali National Park. Traversing forested uplands, broad sweeps of tundra, glacial streams and mountain slopes, the park road is a minor engineering marvel—and a magic carpet that transports visitors into another world.

A bus slowly negotiates hairpin turns on its climb up to the top of Polychrome Overlook, Denali National Park.

FAIRBANKS

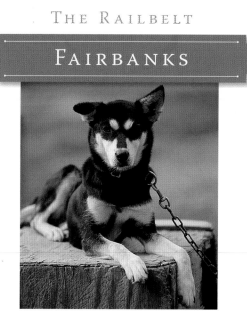

F AIRBANKS DOESN'T PUT ON AIRS. Though it ranks a distant second in size to Anchorage, and lags far behind in skyline and cosmopolitan savoir-faire, few residents seem to notice—or even faintly care. Sprawling ever outward from its birthplace along the Chena River, this city of 50,000-plus (with another 50 or so in the surrounding North Star Borough area) radiates a no-non-sense, frontier aura befitting its role: the undisputed gateway to Alaska's great Interior, and the Arctic beyond. Gold miners and homesteaders, bush village residents, wilderness adventurers, geologists, dog mushers, oil field workers, hunting guides and their clients—all pass through Fairbanks on their way into the fabled expanse of Alaska's Bush. So do their groceries, fuel, and other supplies. From the central hub of Fairbanks, connecting roads rapidly become fewer and thinner; only the Dalton Highway, the lifeline to the Prudhoe Bay oil fields, leads beyond the Yukon River.

(above) An Interior Alaska sled dog sits on top of its dog house.
(left) A farm worker feeds musk-ox at the Large Animal Research
Station in Fairbanks run by the University of Alaska Fairbanks.

Paralleling the Alaska Pipeline north of Fairbanks, the Dalton Highway cuts north to Prudhoe Bay and the Arctic Ocean.

FAIRBANKS

The Alaska Railroad makes its turnaround at Fairbanks, too. From there on, the main travel routes are the rivers themselves; overland trails, for the most part passable only in winter; and the invisible threads of air routes traversed by bush planes.

Constellations of Native villages lie scattered wide and far across the land—Athapaskan Indian along the Yukon and Tanana valleys, and Inupiat Eskimo farther north. For these people, caught between the space age and ancient tradition, subsistence hunting, fishing, and gathering are still a way of life. At the same time, they depend on goods and services funneled through Fairbanks.

Like Ketchikan, Fairbanks owes its existence to the single-minded vision of one man—in this case, an entrepreneur by the name of E.T. Barnette. But Barnette and Fairbanks received a huge nudge from both nature and fate as well. In autumn of 1901 Barnette chartered a heavily loaded stern-wheel steamboat northeast up the Yukon, intent on establishing the Interior's major trading post at a strategic location on the upper Tanana River. Thwarted by low water, he, his wife, several employees, and 130 tons of freight ended up stranded on the banks of the Chena, dozens of miles short of their goal.

Though Barnette considered his location no more than a winter camp and a temporary setback, two local gold prospectors gave him some business, and proceeded to strike paydirt the following year. The ensuing rush, though modest compared to others of the period, proved steady—enough to convince Barnette to establish his dream town right there, on the banks of the Chena. In the interest of hastening development, he spread shameless exaggerations of the strike and even "salted" a local claim for the benefit of a credulous visitor. Experienced miners, nonetheless, found rich enough pay streaks to warrant intensive development, even as more distant strikes drew prospectors through town and onward.

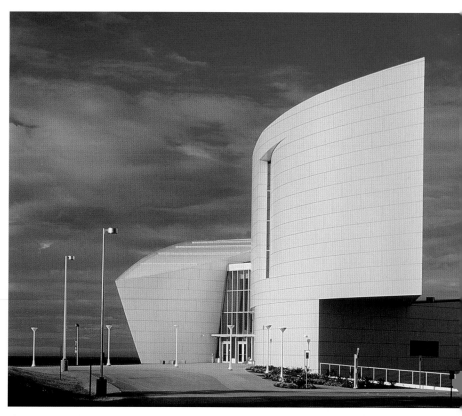

The new wing of the University of Alaska Museum of the North opened in September 2005.

(left) Alaska's "Unknown First Family" sculpture is the centerpiece of downtown Fairbanks' Golden Heart Plaza.

By 1906 Fairbanks had without question grown into the hub Barnette envisioned. The population had mushroomed past 6,000 (several times that of Anchorage), growing in proportion to the annual take of gold—which peaked that year at over $9 million. Several bridges spanned the Chena, and amenities included an electric power plant, phone service, water mains, and sidewalks. A jewelry store, two meat markets, a paint and wallpaper store, and a steam laundry punctuated the fact that Fairbanks had become more than a temporary wide spot on the river bank. A district court, hospital, several churches, and two public schools provided services to the region. Fleets of shallow-draft stern wheel riverboats—the largest capable of carrying 150 passengers and hundreds of tons of freight—plied the Yukon and the Tanana drainages. Fairbanks, with its central location, steadily growing population, and rapidly developing infrastructure,

Paddle wheels of riverboat "Discovery III" churn up the silt-laden waters of Nenana River.

became the main port of call between the distant west coast of Alaska and the Canadian border. Goods of all sorts, from fresh bananas and butter to silk petticoats, mining machinery, and motor cars journeyed thousands of miles from Outside to Fairbanks.

The brief ice-free season (June through early October) and competition from the new Alaska Railroad brought the brief, colorful heyday of the Alaska riverboat to a close by 1920. But even in this era of turbine bush planes, tug-driven freight barges still ply the Yukon and Tanana, and visitors can relive the era on the authentic sternwheeler *Discovery III*, operated as a day excursion boat by the Binkley family, who trace their riverboating experience back four generations.

While Fairbanksians will proudly and definitively point out that their town is no Anchorage, its growth in the past 30 years has been little short of explosive. The oil boom of the 1970s, two large military bases, and a resurgence in large-scale gold mining in the region help drive today's economy, and the University of Alaska Fairbanks, renowned for its engineering and science programs, continues to expand. An active fine arts calendar and an excellent as well as architecturally magnificent new museum bespeak a cultural flair behind the Alaska Casual Carhart-coverall-and-thermal-boot ambiance. Shakespeare, poetry slams, and Swan Lake compete shoulder to shoulder with dog sled races, moose hunting, and the annual sandhill crane migration.

And the future? With a major gas pipeline project and the continuing expansion westward of oil and mineral development in the Arctic (in addition to its ever-expanding role as a regional service community), Fairbanks seems poised to leap forward once again. As always, the next gold rush lies somewhere just beyond.

Riverboat, "Discovery III", Chena River, Fairbanks

ARCTIC NATIONAL WILDLIFE REFUGE

Rafters paddle the Kongakut River towards the Arctic Ocean in the Arctic National Wildlife Refuge.

DRYAS, A COMMON TUNDRA PLANT

ARCTIC NATIONAL WILDLIFE REFUGE

THE NAME ITSELF ECHOES WITH MAGIC: the Arctic National Wildlife Refuge. This vast, distant landscape, in the far upper right-hand corner of the state, embodies Alaska's wilderness at its most pristine. The world of highways, cruise ships, and big-box stores lies far to the south; the only human habitation in more than 19 million acres, three tiny Native villages and a few homesteads, seem lost in an infinite, rolling sea of land.

Straddling the eastern Brooks Range and spilling out across the Arctic Coastal Plain to the edge of the Beaufort Sea, the Refuge (often known as ANWR) ranks among the world's premier natural reserves. Among protected circumpolar lands, its wildlife diversity is unmatched, ranging from polar bears and musk oxen to more than 150 species of migratory birds from four continents. During the fleeting arctic spring and summer, the Porcupine caribou herd, 50,000 strong, gathers in huge concentrations, reminiscent of Africa's Serengeti. Many of these same animals cross into Canada on their annual migration. The Refuge is a place that transcends borders or politics.

By Alaska standards, the land itself verges on the austere. No tidewater glaciers rumble, no immense rain forest trees reach skyward; and the tallest mountains, though imposing, could be swallowed in Denali's shadow. The beauty of the Arctic Refuge, like the rest of Alaska's far north remains, for the most part, subtle—yet profound as a distant wolf howl. The summer sun's parabolic, horizon-lapping course, combined with a startling clarity of the air itself, casts the world in ever-shifting tones that distort the fabric of time and space itself. Mountains miles away seem close enough to touch. Thousands of caribou appear as if conjured out of air, then vanish just as abruptly. At times, the silence is so complete that your own heartbeat echoes within it.

(preceding pages 152-153) With the Brooks Range in the background, thousands of caribou form large summer aggregations for protection from insects and predators on the coastal plain near the Beaufort Sea, in the Arctic National Wildlife Refuge.

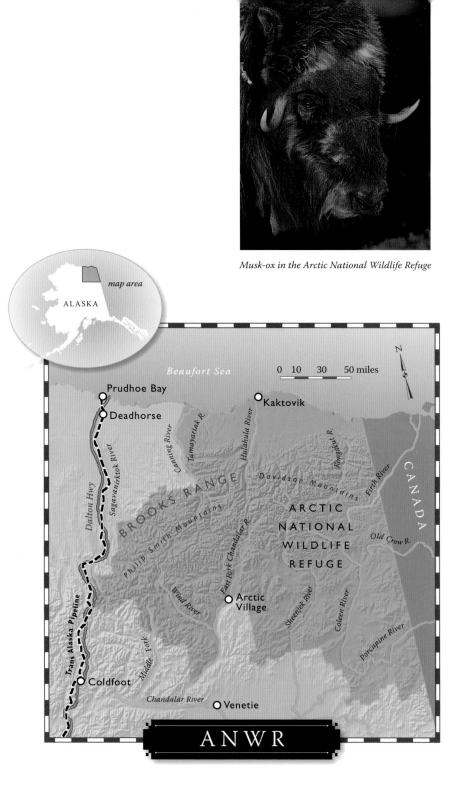

Musk-ox in the Arctic National Wildlife Refuge

map area

ALASKA

Beaufort Sea

0 10   30   50 miles

N

Prudhoe Bay

Kaktovik

Deadhorse

Tamayariak R.

Canning River

Hulahula River

Kongakut R.

Dalton Hwy

Sagavanirktok River

Davidson Mountains

Firth River

CANADA

BROOKS RANGE

ARCTIC

Philip Smith Mountains

East Fork Chandalar R.

NATIONAL

WILDLIFE

Old Crow R.

REFUGE

Wind River

Arctic
Village

Sheenjek River

Coleen River

Trans Alaska Pipeline

Middle Fork

Porcupine River

Coldfoot

Chandalar River

Venetie

ANWR

ARCTIC NATIONAL WILDLIFE REFUGE

For many people, this ethereal landscape has come to symbolize wild Alaska itself, and its fate, that of the whole. And indeed, the decades-long, heated debate over oil drilling on the Refuge's coastal plain drags onward with no certain end in sight. But pressures on Alaska's wilderness, once so vast as to seem both infinite and eternal, continue to mount. Ninety-five percent of Alaska's Arctic Slope remains open to oil drilling (which, very quietly, is expanding at an unprecedented pace westward through equally fragile and profound wilderness). From Southeast Alaska to Southcentral, in Southwest, through the Interior and across the entire Arctic, development projects (most aimed at extractive resources including oil, gas, coal, other minerals, and timber) are either ongoing or in initial stages. The grids for the roads and railroads of tomorrow already crisscross the planning maps of today. What is some desolate mountain valley—scenic though it might be—when untold billions of dollars lie there, waiting to be scooped up? Pro-development voices assure us of responsible development and redundant environmental safeguards. And, they say, there's enough land for everyone, including the caribou and bears.

As you travel this great land and marvel at its scenic wonders, imagine the Alaska you'd like your grandchildren, and their children, to see. If it's still there a century from now, it will only be because enough people—citizens of the world as well as Alaskans—raised their voices and willed it so, not once but many times. May there always be such a place far and away, large enough to hold all our dreams.

Caribou cross the Tamayariak River on the coastal plain of the Arctic National Wildlife Refuge.

SPECIAL THANKS

SPECIAL THANKS goes to Nick Jans and Laura Lucas for their incredible talents and their dedication to making this book possible. Thanks to my wife, Jan, and sons, Gabe and Owen, for putting up with my overwhelming work and travel schedule and for all the fun and love they bring to my life. I could have never done this book with out Charity Green, my business manager, taking over the business and cutting me loose to photograph. Along the way, so many people helped me in so many ways. I'd like to acknowledge them and thank them for their efforts. If you helped me out and you are not listed here, please accept my apologies and know I appreciated your efforts.

☞ MARK KELLEY

Ketchikan Visitors Bureau • Allen Marine Tours, Ketchikan
Michelle Madsen with Island Wings Air Service, Ketchikan
Laurie Booyse & Tia Weary with Allen Marine Tours, Ketchikan
Leslie Chapel with Ketchikan Visitors Bureau
Jolene Winther with Madame's Manor Bed and Breakfast, Ketchikan
Sitka Convention & Visitors Bureau • Sitka Hotel
Sandy Lorrigan with Sitka Convention & Visitors Bureau
Allen Marine Tours, Sitka • John Dunlap with Allen Marine Tours, Sitka
Sherry Aitken & Jason Dineen with Allen Marine Tours, Sitka
Jim Collins with Allen Marine Tours, Juneau • Tim McDonnell with Temsco, Juneau
Lorene Palmer with Juneau Convention and Visitors Bureau
Bob Jacobson with Wings of Alaska, Juneau
Paul Johnson, Tami Mulick, Rick Johnson & Alice Johnson with Gull Cove Lodge
Joe Giefer, Karey Cooperrider & Christine Giefer
with Admiralty Wilderness Lodge, Funter Bay, Admiralty Island
David Riccio with Lemon Creek Digital, Juneau • Terra Dawn Parker, Juneau
Larry Persily, Anchorage • Phillips Cruises & Tours, Whittier
Capt. Thomas Lee & Capt. Nina Pere Himmelwright with Phillips Cruises & Tours in Whittier
Barrie Swanberg & Marsha Barton with Phillips Cruises & Tours
Tougas Family: Tom, Mary, Paul, Melissa, & Rachel
Renown Tours, Seward • Herman "Howie" Leite, Seward
Captain Mark Lindstrom, Seward
Karen Stomberg & Areli Miller, Fairbanks • Will Schendel, Fairbanks
Camp Denali, Denali National Park
Simon & Jenna Hamm with Camp Denali, Denali National Park
Todd Sherman, Fairbanks • Alaska Discovery, Juneau • Jeff Sloss with Alaska Discovery
Ken Leghorn & Susan Warner, Juneau

Dwarf fireweed, also known as "river beauties,"
Granite Creek Basin, Juneau

Photo by Owen Kelley

MARK KELLEY

Mark Kelley is one of Alaska's most published photographers with his photographs appearing as covers on more than 200 publications. He has created and published a series of books, calendars, note cards, and postcards over the years. *Alaska: A Photographic Excursion* is his ninth book. Mark has lived in Alaska for more than 30 years and resides in Juneau with his wife, Jan, two sons, Gabe and Owen, and family dog, Rosie. To see more of his work go to his website at www.markkelley.com

PHOTOGRAPHER'S NOTES

I started photographing Alaska after arriving in Fairbanks to attend the University of Alaska in August 1974. This book is the culmination of 30-plus years of photography passion for everything Alaska. A few of the photos came from the 70s, but most were shot in the last five years, with 70 of the images taken during the final summer of shooting before the publication of this book.

I shot the photographs in this book using Nikon F5 cameras and a wide range of lenses, including: 20-35mm, 28-75mm, 70-200mm, and 80-400mm zooms; and both 300mm and 500mm telephotos. Most of the photos were shot using Fuji Velvia slide film. I used graduated neutral density filters and polarizing filters on occasion.

Editorial honesty is important to me. Except for some very minor retouching, none of the photos in this book have been substantially altered. What you see is what I saw in the viewfinder. All of the photos of wildlife were shot in the places that they appear in the book. I did not use a photo of an animal from one part of the state to represent another part of the state.

I hope you enjoy the book. Thanks.
☞ *Mark Kelley*

This book won the national 2008 *Benjamin Franklin Award* as one of the best books published in the USA in 2007. The Independent Book Publishers Association represents over 4,000 publishers and sponsors this annual award which is in its 20th year. Over 1,800 books were entered in the 2007 contest with this book winning the regional category.

Photo by Mark Kelley

NICK JANS

Writer/photographer Nick Jans is a contributing editor to *Alaska Magazine* and a member of *USA Today's* board of editorial contributors. He has also written six books on Alaska wilderness, including *The Grizzly Maze: Timothy Treadwell's Fatal Obsession With Alaskan Bears* and *Tracks of the Unseen: Meditations on Alaska Wildlife, Landscape, and Photography*, as well as more than 200 articles, opinion pieces, and poems published in a variety of magazines, books, and newspapers, from the Japanese language arts journal *Switch* to *Rolling Stone*. He's won a number of regional and national writing awards, most recently as a co-recipient of a 2006 Ben Franklin award with photographer Mark Kelley and designer Laura Lucas for the small-format photography book, *Alaska's Tracy Arm*. A 20-year resident of Iñupiaq villages in Northwest Arctic Alaska, Nick currently makes his home in Juneau with his wife Sherrie, three dogs, two parrots, an orphan hummingbird or squirrel or mink now and then, and whatever else shows up.